THE PSALMS:
SINGING VERSION

This widely praised translation of the Psalms is the work of a team of scholars in co-operation with *The Grail*. It was inspired by the work of R. Tourney, o.p., Raymond Schwab, J. Gelineau, s.j. and T. G. Chifflot, o.p., who were responsible for the translation of the *Bible de Jérusalem* Psalms from Hebrew into French and had the happy thought of bringing the rhythmic pattern of the Hebrew into their rendering. The Grail would like to record their debt to these four French scholars.

In this Singing Version, the musical psalm formulas of Joseph Gelineau are included, together with detailed instructions for making use of this new method of singing. There are also notes on the Christian significance of each psalm by Fr. Alexander Jones, editor of the forthcoming translation of the *Bible de Jérusalem*, and by Fr. Leonard Johnston.

THE PSALMS

**A NEW TRANSLATION FROM THE
HEBREW ARRANGED FOR SINGING
TO THE PSALMODY OF
JOSEPH GELINEAU**

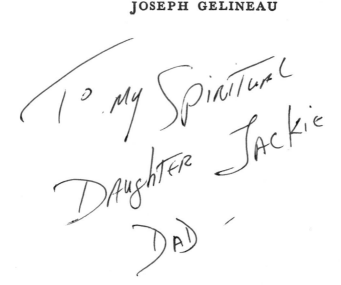

To my Spiritual
Daughter Jackie
Dad

PAULIST PRESS
New York / Mahwah

3
2018

INTRODUCTION

1. The Songs of Israel

The 150 poems which make up the book of psalms sing to us the human and divine history of Israel.

A psalm is a religious song. The very word 'psalm' suggests a musical instrument, tambourine or sistrum, harp or primitive lyre, with which the singer accompanied his song. The psalmist recited the verses to a simple chant, some echoes of which can doubtless be heard in certain Jewish and Christian psalmodies. These verses showed a balanced symmetry of form and sense, they scanned rhythmically in three, four or five feet, and were linked in more or less frequent stanzas. When he speaks a whole world of images rises from his words as they call to each other, repeating, following or clashing with each other. He makes his point not by reasoning but by hammering; he reveals not by describing but by actually touching; he teaches not by explaining but by putting his words on our lips.

The psalms are a series of shouts: shouts of love and hatred; shouts of suffering or rejoicing; shouts of faith or hope. Here, a man who has suffered injury demands justice (Psalm 55) or the whole defeated nation laments (Psalm 43); there, a sick man who has escaped death gives thanks (Psalm 29) or the whole people proclaim that the hand of God alone has rescued them from foreign slavery (Psalm 80). Wise men meditate on the Law, the charter of the covenant between God and his people (Psalm 118), and choirs celebrate the power and holiness of the Lord who overthrows the strong and raises up the humble (Psalm 146).

How were these poems born? Where, when and by whom were they written? Tradition attributes them to King David 'the singer of the songs of Israel' (2 Sam. 23: 1) or to the musicians' guilds connected with the names of Asaph or Korah. There is no doubt that the psalm *genre* goes back very far in the history of Israel and that David

5

excelled in the art. Nevertheless it is no longer possible to attach a date or author to each psalm. This is less important than the fact that Israel has preserved these poems because it has recognised in them the expression of its unique religious destiny. The psalms repeat in lyrical form the teaching of the prophets; they recall the great events of a history that was itself a divine revelation; they meditate on the covenant.

The collection of the psalms into five books was possibly made for liturgical purposes. It was compiled after the return from the Babylonian captivity and was completed by the third century before Christ. A great number of the psalms belong to this post-exile period, but some are clearly earlier, and recall the period of the Kings (e.g. Psalms 19-20). In the controversial matter of psalm chronology, we should forget neither the enduring character of an age-old literary form, which lends itself to creative imitation, nor the progressive nature of a revelation which continued to inform the ancient formulas with an ever clearer messianic consciousness.

2. Prophecy and Christ's Prayer

On Easter night, when the redemption had been accomplished in the death and resurrection of Christ, Jesus said to his apostles: 'This is what I told you while I still walked in your company; how all that was written of me in the law of Moses, and in the prophets, and in the psalms, must be fulfilled' (Luke 24: 44). In Christ the full significance of the songs of Israel is revealed; they announced the Word of Life. He personally described himself as the Lord whom God seated at his right hand (Psalm 109, Matt. 22: 44); as the stone rejected by the builders which became the head of the corner (Psalm 117, Matt. 21: 42); as he who comes, blessed in the name of the Lord (Psalm 117, Matt. 23: 39). He personally applied to himself on the cross the appeal of the persecuted psalmist (Psalm 21, Matt. 27: 46) and his prayer of trust (Psalm 30, Luke 23: 46).

Everything that the psalms had sung about Yahweh the God of Israel, as the one who judges and saves his people, who comes to dwell among them, who reveals his Law to them, gathers them together, leads and sanctifies them, all that finds its expression and its accomplishment in the Incarnate Word. Since then we know the 'Lord' of the psalms and 'have seen his glory': it is Jesus the Son of David and the Son of God, who judges the world in his death, who saves it in his resurrection, who has become man among us and has made the Father known to us; he is the Truth, the Way and the Life of which the psalms speak.

God and Saviour, Jesus is also the Son of Man, recapitulating in the passover of his death and resurrection the whole destiny of mankind. The appeal of the just man under persecution and the cry of the suffering servant are more fitting on his lips than on those of any of the afflicted people of Israel; and his resurrection gives more meaning to redeemed humanity's song of thanksgiving than any short-lived delivery from evil in the Old Testament. The psalms, expressing as they do man's attitude before God, find the fullness of their meaning in the new Adam. Henceforth we recognise in Christ the God of the psalms. Henceforth the voice of the psalmist is the voice of Christ.

3. The Psalms in the Preaching and the Prayer of the Church

Enlightened by the Spirit of Pentecost the apostles saw the mysteries of Christ foreshadowed in these inspired poems. In their preaching Peter and Paul used these familiar texts to show that what they pointed to had been fulfilled in the risen Christ (Acts 2: 25-35; Acts 13: 33; Eph. 4: 8, etc.). All their successors—Justin, Hippolytus, Hilary, Augustine—give the psalms the same privileged place in their preaching of the Gospel. All the Christian liturgies make the psalter their first source for texts to celebrate the mysteries of the Lord, his birth (Psalm 2: 7); his manifestation to the Gentiles (Psalm 97: 2); his sufferings and death (Psalm 21); his resurrection (Psalm 117); his ascension (Psalm 46), and his second coming to judge all men (Psalm 95).

It is not surprising therefore that Christ's Church should have found in the psalms her favourite prayer. These inspired verses resound in the liturgy of the Word, in the

7

celebration of the Mass, in the Divine Office, and in the most varied ceremonies of every rite. The Bride delights to use the words of the Spirit. At one moment she uses them to praise her heavenly Lord, at another she identifies her voice with that of the mediator, the true and universal psalmist, in order to pray to the Father. Yet again she turns towards Christ, God made man, to ask for help or to give him thanks.

For the Church is the new Israel and the new people of God. As the Body of the risen Christ, she is the true Temple; as the assembly of believers, she is the new Jerusalem. Through the images of the old covenant the Church gives voice to the invisible realities of the new covenant.

4. The Psalms in our Prayer

'We were born with this book in our very bones. A small book; 150 poems; 150 steps between death and life; 150 mirrors of our rebellions and our loyalties, of our agonies and our resurrections. More than a book, it is a living being who speaks, who suffers, groans and dies, who rises again and speaks on the threshold of eternity; who seizes one, bears one away, oneself and all the ages of time, from the beginning to the end' (A. Chouraqi).

No one who takes the words of the psalms on his lips and their meaning in his heart, who allows the rhythm of their images to take hold of him and their accents to echo through his being, can possibly remain indifferent to them. They may overwhelm or shock, bring peace or exaltation, but inevitably they draw us beyond ourselves; they force us to that meeting with the God without whom we cannot live and who transforms our whole life. The psalms compel us to belief and hope.

Some may object that certain passages contradict the command of love taught us by Christ. But we have only to follow the images through to their Easter fulfilment in Christ's passover, and to ask ourselves what it is that the psalmist loves and hates, to realise that the choice no longer lies between friends or enemies, but between the reign of evil which holds sway in us and the reign of grace which lays claim to us. If these words leave us unmoved it means

8

that we are incapable of hatred and consequently of love. If they are a stumbling block for us, it means that the man of the Old Testament is still sleeping within us though we claim to be disciples of Christ.

Others raise different objections: they don't care to join the psalmist in proclaiming their own innocence or loyalty; they don't want to pray in terms of an anguish they have not experienced, or give thanks with a jubilation they have never felt. But do such people think that the prayers they use are merely their own prayers? Do they not realise that they stand before God in the company of the whole of mankind? Their prayer is that of the whole Church and it only reaches the Father through the voice of Christ the Mediator. The psalms compel us to voice all the prayer of the people of God and of their Head; they force us to widen our hearts to the full dimensions of the redemption. They make us say what remains hidden except to the eyes of faith, and what we know we must one day become.

5. Ancient and Modern Versions

God speaks to man in human words. The revelation contained in holy Scripture can only reach the men to whom it is addressed if it uses the languages they speak.

More than two centuries before Christ the book of psalms was translated into Greek in Alexandria. This Septuagint version was used by the authors of the New Testament for their preaching of Christianity, and it continued to serve as a basis for most of the ancient translations of the psalms, in particular for the most widespread of the Latin versions, known as the Vulgate. It is readily understandable that the Septuagint continues to retain a special authority in the Church.

However, as a result of progress in biblical studies, almost all modern versions of the psalms are today based on the original text. This recourse to the Hebrew allows the translator to stay close to this unique literary form, with its repetition of words, its own particular images, its stylistic peculiarities and its poetic rhythm. The translation of a poem cannot be made simply by a faithful rendering of its meaning. The whole character of the original language must be conveyed. When it is a matter of the word of God, where the historical nature of revelation has made content and form even more inseparable, the need for literary fidelity takes on special importance; though this does not mean that the ancient versions may be neglected, witnessing as they do to the way in which the Church has interpreted the inspired text.

It is this literary fidelity which was aimed at in the French Version of the *Bible de Jérusalem* (1st edition by R. Tournay and R. Schwab, Paris 1950; 2nd edition with the collaboration of J. Gelineau and T. G. Chifflot, Paris 1955). Special attention was paid to the rhythmic structure of the poetry of the psalms, and this allowed a sung or recited psalmody to be fashioned on the basis of the analogy that exists between the Hebrew tonic rhythm and that of our modern languages.

Since 1953 this new way of singing the psalms has spread rapidly among French Catholics. Following the success of the French venture, The Grail took the initiative in making an English translation based on the same principles. The work was begun in 1954 with the collaboration of Gall Schuon, o.c.s.o., Albert Derzelle, o.c.s.o., and Hubert Richards, l.s.s., for the translation from the original texts, of Philippa Craig for the literary style, and (in the musical editions) of Gregory Murray, o.s.b. for the 'singability'. The first collection of 24 psalms appeared in 1956 and a further collection of 30 psalms in 1958, both collections being arranged for singing. The whole 150 have now been translated and appear in this volume. From the efforts of this team has come a translation which Professor H. H. Rowley has described as 'a very impressive rendering' for which he has 'nothing but praise'.

At a time when those who profess Jesus Christ as their only Saviour are searching for the things that will end their separation and unite them, may the inspired poetry of the psalms allow all of them to sing in the same words and in the same Spirit their common faith in the same Lord.

J. GELINEAU

GELINEAU PSALMODY

As already explained, this translation of the psalms follows the example of the French *Bible de Jérusalem* in reproducing the literary forms of the orignal Hebrew in addition to its meaning. The Psalms are therefore set out in stanzas of different lengths, varying from two lines (as in Psalm 116 [117]) to as many as sixteen lines (as in Psalm 118 [119]). Furthermore, the rhythmic pattern of each line of the Hebrew has been reproduced in the translation.

Hebrew verse was organised on an accentual basis. Every line had a stipulated number of accented or stressed syllables, although the total number of syllables in the line was variable. In this respect Hebrew verse employed the same rhythmic principle as early English verse, for which Gerard Manley Hopkins invented the term 'sprung rhythm'. Sprung rhythm, as Hopkins observed, is to be found also in much of our later poetry and frequently occurs in nursery rhymes and popular jingles. A simple instance is to be found in 'Three blind mice'. Each line has 3 stressed syllables and a fourth beat. But the number of syllables in the lines varies between 3 and 11. That all the lines may be sung simultaneously shows that they all have the same rhythmic structure of 4 beats.

Father Gelineau's psalm-tones are designed to fit the varying lengths of stanza of the psalms and the varying rhythmic patterns of the lines. Melodically they are based upon and inspired by ancient psalm-tones from Gregorian, Ambrosian and other sources, and they are written in different 'modes' of the diatonic scale.

As the pages of psalm-tones at the back of the book show, there are six groups of tones. Groups I, II and III are for stanzas of 4 lines; groups IV, V and VI are for stanzas of 6 lines. But provision is made for irregular stanzas in which the number of lines is abnormal.

In the psalms every line has either 4, 3 or 2 stressed syllables, indicated in the present book by accents. The most frequent pattern is the 3-stress line, employed in the first three psalms. Psalm 4 illustrates the least common pattern, the 4-stress line. The frequent pattern of alternate lines of 3-stress and 2-stress may be seen in Psalm 5.

Each psalm-tone has its lines marked with capital letters: A, B, C, etc. Every line begins with a measure containing a rest followed by a black note. This introductory measure is to accommodate syllables occurring before the first stress of the line, and such introductory syllables are to be sung on the black note. Where the line begins with a stress without introductory syllables, the introductory measure is silent for the singers, only the accompaniment being heard. In other words the introductory measure is never omitted.

The pace at which the psalms are to be sung is controlled by a fairly slow beat coinciding with the beginning of each measure and with the stressed syllables. These beats should occur with rigid regularity. The extra beat at the beginning of each measure (for introductory syllables) means that for a 4-stress line there are 5 beats, for a 3-stress line there are 4 beats, and for a 2-stress line there are 3 beats—much as in the 3-stress lines of 'Three blind mice' there are 4 beats, except that in the psalms the extra beat comes at the beginning of the line, not at the end.

The timing of the stressed syllables to coincide with the regular beats presents no great problem. In singing the psalms it is not necessary, in fact it would be inartistic, to mark the stressed syllables by heavy accentuation. They acquire all the emphasis they need by coinciding with the beats. It is chiefly in the matter of the intervening syllables that difficulties are sometimes experienced. These intervening syllables should be sung with the natural rhythm of careful speech. The speed at which these intervening syllables are sung will depend on their number: 3 syllables occurring between 2 beats will obviously be sung more quickly than 1 or 2. But the variations in the speed of intervening syllables must not be allowed to interfere with their basic speech-rhythm.[1]

Occasionally the main note in a measure is followed by one or two black notes, as, for instance, in tone 42 of

[1] Suggestions for the treatment of intervening syllables are offered in a booklet obtainable from The Grail, 58 Sloane Street, London, s.w.1, entitled *Grail-Gelineau Psalms* (6d.).

group I, in tone 31 of group II, in tone 34 of group III. The last one or two intervening syllables are sung to these black notes, but the subsequent beat is not delayed.

In this edition every psalm is marked with a suitable psalm-tone reference. Thus for Psalm 1 the tone suggested is v 55, i.e. tone 55 in group v. Any other tone in this group would fit the psalm, but it was necessary to suggest specific psalm-tones in order that antiphons might be provided in the same mode and tonality.

These antophons, to be published separately, form an important, though not essential, element in Gelineau Psalmody. Their purpose is to provide simple refrains for a congregation to sing between the stanzas of a psalm, the psalm itself being sung by a soloist or a choir. The varied uses of the antiphons are explained in the published musical editions.

It will be seen that some of the psalms—e.g. 22 [23], 116 [117], 118 [119], 135 [136], 136 [137], 148—are not allocated to ordinary psalm-tones given in the six groups. Their proper music may be found in the published musical editions to which reference is made.[2] Ps 24 = *Twenty-Four Psalms and a Canticle*; Ps 30 = *Thirty Psalms and two Canticles*; Ps 20 = *Twenty Psalms and Two Canticles*.[3] But some of these psalms could be sung to the regular psalm-tones. Thus Psalm 118 [119], which has stanzas of 16 lines, could be sung in 4-line stanzas to any of the psalm-tones in group I. And Psalm 22 [23] could be sung to any of the tones in group IV, allowance being made for the initial line of the first stanza which has only 2 stresses instead of the normal 3.

A word should be added concerning the popular setting of this Psalm 22 [23] given in *Twenty-Four Psalms and a Canticle*. This, as Father Gelineau has explained, was a first attempt to provide a musical setting for a psalm and it is not really typical of Gelineau Psalmody. It is melodic in

---

[2] Unless the stanzas of a psalm are thus separated by the congregational singing of an antiphon, the stanzas themselves should be sung alternately by two choirs or by soloist and choir. That stanza after stanza should be sung by the same singers without interruption is a procedure to be discouraged. Occasionally, however, an entire psalm might be sung by a soloist as a meditative reading to the assembly.

[3] All these musical editions, and others, may be obtained from The Grail, 58 Sloane Street, London, s.w.1, as well as various gramophone recordings of the psalms.

character rather than recitative, and to that extent it falls short as an ideal psalm-tone. Moreover it is clearly in duple time, with two clearly marked beats in the measure. In this respect the setting differs fundamentally from the psalm-tones in the six groups. When these tones are employed it is most important to avoid introducing more than one beat in each measure. If secondary beats are introduced, implied or suggested, the speech-rhythm of the intervening syllables will almost certainly be impaired. For the regular psalm-tones, therefore, the principle of one (fairly slow) beat in the measure must be scrupulously maintained.

A. GREGORY MURRAY

Note. Sometimes when the last stanza of a psalm is two lines shorter than the normal stanza, the stanza is completed by adding the shorter form of doxology in the appropriate rhythm. The need for this is indicated by (*Doxology*).

NOTES ON THE PSALMS

Fr. Alexander Jones, editor of the forthcoming translation of the *Jerusalem Bible*, and Fr. Leonard Johnston have provided notes on the Christian significance of each psalm for this Singing Version.

A NOTE ON THE NUMBERING OF THE PSALMS AND VERSES

The numbering of the psalms to be found in most Christian liturgies is taken from the Greek Septuagint. This numeration differs from that found in the Hebrew text and the Authorised Version. Since books with a liturgical emphasis (such as the present one) generally follow the Septuagint numbering, and other Biblical and exegetical works the Hebrew, it seems useful to give the comparative numbering of the two systems:

Greek Septuagint	Hebrew
1-8	1-8
9	9-10
10-112	11-113
113	114-115
114-115	116
116-145	117-146
146-147	147
148-150	148-150

Therefore for most of the pslams the Greek numeration is one behind that of the Hebrew.

The numbering of the verses is also slightly different from that of the later English version. These generally begin numbering the verses from the body of the psalm, and leave its preceding title out of account. The liturgical texts on the other hand have included the title in their reckoning, and when this is more than a few words long, they have counted the beginning of the psalm as its second or third verse. It is this latter system which has been followed here, though the wording of the titles themselves has not been included. Very occasionally the sequence of verses within a psalm has been disturbed (as for instance in psalm 21: 16-18) in an attempt to restore what appears to have been the order of the original.

I

Two ways of living

A study in black and white as a prelude to the whole psalter. The sharp contrast between the virtuous and the wicked is characteristic of Hebrew thought and its uncompromising literary expression. This is not to say that the psalmist was unconscious of the mixture of good and bad to be found in himself and in others around him. As St. Paul was to say much later —and he spoke for everyone—'though the will to do what is good is in me, the performance is not'. Aware of this tension in ourselves we could hardly recite this psalm without a feeling of hypocrisy, were it not that this is no proclamation of one's own virtue but a constant self-reminder. We may never reach the extremes either of virtue or of vice, but we are at every moment making for one or the other, and it is salutary to remind ourselves what the end of each road is. It is better still to remember that we have a powerful companion along the one road, but along the other we are alone.

FORMULA V 55

1 Háppy indéed is the mán
who fóllows not the cóunsel of the wícked;
nor língers in the wáy of sínners
nor síts in the cómpany of scórners,
2 but whose delíght is the láw of the Lórd
and who pónders his láw day and níght.

3 Hé is like a trée that is plánted
besíde the flówing wáters,
that yíelds its frúit in due séason
and whose léaves shall néver fáde;
and áll that he dóes shall prósper.
4 Not só are the wícked, not só!

For théy like wínnowed cháff
shall be dríven awáy by the wínd.
5 When the wícked are júdged they shall not stánd,
nor find róom among thóse who are júst;
6 for the Lórd guards the wáy of the júst
but the wáy of the wícked leads to dóom.

17

2

The Messianic kingship: warning to rulers and nations

Temple and palace stood side by side on Zion, God's arm supported the sceptre of the anointed Davidic king, his 'Christ'. On this same hill our Lord declared himself both Temple and King—shrine of the Godhead and ruler of the world. The earliest Church, therefore, seized upon our psalm: 'Jesus is the victorious anointed of David's stock' (Acts 4: 25ff); he rules 'with a rod of iron . . . and on his armour is written "King of kings"' (Apoc. 19: 16). The victory is won not by this world's kings (by Antipas and Pilate), not by the 'princes' or leaders of Israel, but by the one they crucified (Acts 4: 26-7). The persecution of Christians and the passion of Christ are one and the same (Acts 4: 29), and the victory of resurrection is equally assured. On Christian lips our psalm is a song of defiance—defiance of the spirit in the name of God.

1 Whý this túmult among nátions,
    among péoples this úseless múrmuring?
2 They aríse, the kíngs of the éarth,
    princes plót against the Lórd and his Anóinted.
3 'Cóme, let us bréak their fétters,
    cóme, let us cást off their yóke.'

4 He who síts in the héavens láughs;
    the Lórd is láughing them to scórn.
5 Thén he will spéak in his ánger,
    his ráge will stríke them with térror.
6 'It is Í who have sét up my kíng
    on Zíon, my hóly móuntain.'

7 (I will annóunce the decrée of the Lórd:)

    The Lórd said to me: 'Yóu are my Són.
    It is Í who have begótten you this dáy.
8 Ásk and I shall bequéath you the nátions,

put the énds of the éarth in your posséssion.
9 With a ród of íron you will bréak them,
shátter them like a pótter's jár.'

10 Nów, O kíngs, understánd,
take wárning, rúlers of the éarth;
11 sérve the Lórd with áwe
and trémbling, páy him your hómage
12 lést he be ángry and you pérish;
for súddenly his ánger will bláze.

Blessed are théy who put their trúst in Gód.

3

Confidence under persecution: a morning prayer

The 'enemies' who appear so often in the psalter are always trying to undermine the psalmist's trust in God, or more exactly the psalmist sees their political or personal hostility as a test of his confidence in the shield that protects him. It follows that though we and the psalmist have different enemies we are fighting in a common cause: to keep the supply-lines open between God and ourselves. Difficulties from outside us and struggles within are not in themselves good things: they are only good as opportunities, or rather as urgent invitations to turn to the only place where help is to be found.

FORMULA II 8

2 How mány are my fóes, O Lórd!
How mány are rísing up agáinst me!
3 How mány are sáying abóut me:
'There is no hélp for hím in Gód.

4 But yóu, Lord, are a shíeld abóut me,
my glóry, who líft up my héad.
5 I crý alóud to the Lórd.
He ánswers from his hóly móuntain.

6 I líe down to rést and I sléep.
I wáke, for the Lórd uphólds me.
7 I will not féar even thóusands of péople
who are ránged on every síde agáinst me.

8 Aríse, Lord; sáve me, my Gód,
you who stríke all my fóes on the móuth,
you who bréak the téeth of the wícked!
9 O Lórd of salvátion, bless your péople!

4

Night prayer

To forget to thank may be bad but to refuse to ask is a thousand times worse, indeed fatal, and this psalmist will not make that mistake: he has learnt from experience. The happiness and peace he knows are lasting and satisfying. Few understand this: the celebrations of harvest-time seem to content them. There is no harm in these things—they are the gifts of God and we enjoy them gratefully: our mistake is in thinking they can satisfy. To be at peace with God is to be at peace with oneself.

FORMULA PS 30

2 When I cáll, ánswer me, O Gód of jústice;
from ánguish you reléased me, have mércy and héar
me!

3 O mén, how lóng will your héarts be clósed,
will you lóve what is fútile and séek what is fálse?

4 It is the Lórd who grants fávours to thóse whom he
lóves;
the Lórd héars me whenéver I cáll him.

5 Fear him; do not sín: pónder on your béd and be stíll.
6 Make jústice your sácrifice and trúst in the Lórd.

7 'What can bríng us háppiness?' mány sáy.
Líft up the líght of your fáce on us, O Lórd.

8 You have pút into my héart a gréater jóy
than théy have from abúndance of córn and new wíne.

9 I will líe down in péace and sléep comes at ónce
for yóu alone, Lórd, make me dwéll in sáfety.

5

Morning prayer

By the mercy of God every new day brings fresh hope to most of us. It would seem that the psalmist has been falsely accused of some crime, and that he is hoping that today at last the accusers will be exposed. In this hope he goes to the Temple to watch and wait for God to intervene. The enemies of God's servants are God's enemies: God will see to them. They may deceive human judges with their honeyed words but not God: he sees the bitterness and the corruption inside. Such indictments as these make us uneasy, if we are thoughtful; in them we often find a portrait of ourselves. At least this consideration is a good general approach to what we might call the 'hostile' psalms.

FORMULA I 15

2 To my wórds give éar, O Lórd,
give héed to my gróaning.
3 Atténd to the sóund of my críes,
my Kíng and my Gód.

It is yóu whom I invóke, *4* O Lórd.
In the mórning you héar me;
in the mórning I óffer you my práyer,
wátching and wáiting.

5 Yóu are no Gód who loves évil;
no sínner is your guést.
6 The bóastful shall not stánd their gróund
befóre your fáce.

7 You háte áll who do évil:
you destróy all who líe.

The decéitful and blóodthirsty mán
the Lórd detésts.

8 But Í through the gréatness of your lóve
have áccess to your hóuse.
I bów down befóre your holy témple,
fílled with áwe.

9 Léad me, Lórd, in your jústice,   [omit a]
because of thóse who lie in wáit;
make cléar your way befóre me.

10 No trúth can be fóund in their móuths,
their héart is all míschief,
their thróat a wíde-open gráve,
all hóney their spéech.

11 Decláre them guílty, O Gód.
Let them fáil in their desígns.
Drive them oút for their mány offénces;
for théy have defíed you.

12 All thóse you protéct shall be glád
and ríng out their jóy.
You shélter them; in yóu they rejóice,
those who lóve your náme.

13 It is yóu who bless the júst man, Lórd:
you surróund him with fávour as with a shíeld.

6

Prayer in time of distress:
first psalm of repentance

*This and the 'penitential' Psalm 37 are very similar but here there is not
the same frank confession of guilt: indeed there is no mention of it and
the term 'penitential', though traditional, seems scarcely to apply. The
'anger' and 'rage' of God, like his 'forsaking', may be conventional*

metaphors for the psalmist's suffering. At this stage of revelation there is no hope of praising God beyond the grave: the conclusion should be clear: death would deprive God of one of his servants. The implication is almost impertinent, that God will be the loser if the psalmist dies. May we threaten God in our private prayers? I suppose not, but some of the inspired authors come very near to it. Anyway, let us not be too scrupulous: God knows how awkward we are and that we mean well. He is a Father, not a literary critic.

FORMULA V 3

2 Lórd, do not repróve me in your ánger;
   púnish me nót, in your ráge.
3 Have mércy on me, Lórd, I have no stréngth;
   Lord, héal me, my bódy is rácked;
4 my sóul is rácked with páin.

   But yóu, O Lórd . . . how lóng?
5 Retúrn, Lord, réscue my sóul.
   Sáve me in your mérciful lóve;
6 for in déath nó one remémbers you;
   from the gráve, whó can give you práise?

7 Í am exháusted with my gróaning;
   every níght I drench my píllow with téars;
   I bedéw my béd with wéeping.
8 My éye wastes awáy with gríef;
   I have grown óld surróunded by my fóes.

9 Léave me, all yóu who do évil;
   for the Lórd has héard my wéeping.
10 The Lórd has héard my pléa;
   The Lórd will accépt my práyer.
11 All my fóes will retíre in confúsion,
   fóiled and súddenly confóunded.

7

Appeal to God's justice

*We have no difficulty with the opening of this psalm but the confident pro-
testation of innocence that follows it is frightening: we prefer to invoke
God's mercy rather than invite his strict scrutiny. But perhaps we have
no cause for misgiving. A Christian may confidently boast that he is 'just'
because the righteousness that is the property of God alone is truly and
internally communicated to the Christian. In Christ himself the righteousness of God appears and becomes available to those who have access by
faith and baptism to the power of Christ's resurrection. This is the
'justness' we can boast of when we sing this psalm: 'Let him who boasts
boast in the Lord'.*

FORMULA II 10

2 Lord Gód, I take réfuge in yóu.
   From my pursúer sáve me and réscue me,
3 lest he téar me to píeces like a líon
   and drag me óff with nó one to réscue me.

4 Lord Gód, if my hánds have done wróng,   [v 9]
5 if I have páid back évil for góod,
   I who sáved my unjúst oppréssor:
6 then let my fóe pursúe me and séize me,
   let him trámple my lífe to the gróund
   and láy my sóul in the dúst.

           **   *   ***

7 Lórd, rise úp in your ánger,
   ríse against the fúry of my fóes;
   my God, awáke! Yóu will give júdgment.
8 Let the cómpany of nátions gather róund you,
   taking your séat abóve them on hígh.
9 (The Lórd is júdge of the péoples.)

Give júdgment for me, Lórd; I am júst   [IV 14]
and ínnocent of héart.
10 Put an énd to the évil of the wícked!
Make the júst stand fírm,
you who tést mínd and héart,
O júst Gód!

11 Gód is the shíeld that protécts me,
who saves the úpright of héart.
12 Gód is a júst júdge
slów to ánger;
but he thréatens the wícked every dáy,
13 men who wíll not repént.

   * * *

Gód will shárpen his swórd;   [V 9]
he has bráced his bów and taken áim.
14 For thém he has prepáred deadly wéapons;
he bárbs his árrows with fíre.
15 Here is óne who is prégnant with málice,
conceives évil and bríngs forth líes.

16 He digs a pítfall, dígs it déep;   [II 10]
and in the tráp he has máde he will fáll.
17 His málice will recóil on himsélf;
on his ówn head his víolence will fáll.

   * * *

18 I will thánk the Lórd for his jústice:
I will síng to the Lórd, the Most Hígh.
[*Doxology*]

25

8

Man the viceroy of God

A lyrical reflection on the making and endowment of man: 'Let us make man in our own image . . . let him have dominion over the fish, the birds, the beasts' (Gen. 1: 26). He is little less than a god because he has a share in God's dominion. He is much greater than the stars because, child though he is before the Eternal, he has a voice for praise. For us it is a hymn of wonder that one of ourselves—a son of man—should enjoy the divine attributes of 'glory and honour'; that under his feet should lie all things, including the 'last enemy, death' (Heb. 2: 5-13; 1 Cor. 15: 25f); that man should with him rise to immortality. The first Adam was the admiration of the psalmist. The second is ours.

FORMULA II 18

2 How gréat is your náme, O Lórd our Gód,
through áll the éarth!

Your májesty is práised above the héavens;
3 on the líps of chíldren and of bábes
you have found práise to fóil your énemy,
to sílence the fóe and the rébel.

4 When I see the héavens, the wórk of your hánds,
The móon and the stárs which you arránged,
5 what is mán that you should kéep him in mínd,
mortal mán that you cáre for hím?

6 Yet you have máde him little léss than a gód;
with glóry and hónour you crówned him,
7 gave him pówer over the wórks of your hánd,
put áll things únder his féet.

8 Áll of them, shéep and cáttle,
yes, éven the sávage béasts,
9 bírds of the aír, and físh
that máke their wáy through the wáters.

10 How gréat is your náme, O Lórd our Gód,
through áll the éarth!

9

Gratitude and appeal:
an alphabetical psalm

If God can handle the stars he has no difficulty with the human enemies of the psalmist. The Israelite never doubted this but sometimes we suspect that he thinks God too patient altogether. 'Lord, are we to order fire down from heaven to burn them up?' This is the reaction of earlier days to the enemies of God; but Jesus rebukes James and John for it (Luke 9: 54f). Nevertheless, we have to admire the confidence in the power and vigilance of God that inspires these prayers—the impatience is only the impatience of a child sure of his father's strength. We must wait, we may die waiting: God seems to take no notice; in ourselves and in the world around us truth and goodness always seem to be at a disadvantage: the fall of the dice is against them. But God has the last throw and faith stands by the table watching him.

FORMULA II 48

2 I will práise you, Lórd, with all my héart;
   I will recóunt áll your wónders.
3 I will rejóice in yóu and be glád,
   and sing psálms to your náme, O Most Hígh.

4 Sée how my énemies turn báck,
   how they stúmble and pérish befóre you.
5 You uphéld the jústice of my cáuse;
   you sat enthróned, júdging with jústice.

[III 49]
6 You have chécked the nátions, destróyed the wícked;
   you have wíped out their náme for éver and éver.
7 The fóe is destróyed, etérnally rúined.
   You upróoted their cíties; their mémory has pérished.

8 But the Lórd sits enthróned for éver.   [II 48]
   He has sét up his thróne for júdgment;
9 he will júdge the wórld with jústice,
   he will júdge the péoples with his trúth.

27

10 For the oppréssed let the Lórd be a strónghold,
a strónghold in tímes of distréss.
11 Those who knów your náme will trúst you:
you will néver forsáke those who séek you.

12 Sing psálms to the Lórd who dwells in Zíon.
Procláim his mighty wórks among the péoples;
13 for the Avénger of blóod has remémbered them,
has not forgótten the crý of the póor.

14 Have píty on me, Lórd, see my súfferings,
you who sáve me from the gátes of déath;
15 that I may recóunt áll your práise
at the gátes of the cíty of Zíon
and rejóice in your sáving hélp.   [repeat D]

16 The nátions have fállen in the pít which they máde,
                                                    [III 49]
their féet cáught in the snáre they láid.
17 The Lórd has revéaled himsélf, and given júdgment.
The wícked are snáred in the wórk of their own hánds.

18 Let the wícked go dówn among the déad,   [II 48]
all the nátions forgétful of Gód.
19 for the néedy shall not álways be forgótten
nor the hópes of the póor be in váin.

20 Aríse, Lord, let mén not prevául!
Let the nátions be júdged befóre you.
21 Lórd, stríke them with térror,
let the nátions knów they are but mén.

(*Here, in the Hebrew text, Psalm 10 begins*)

1 Lórd, whý do you stánd afar óff   [III 49]
and híde yoursélf in tímes of distréss?
2 The póor man is devóured by the príde of the wícked:
he is cáught in the schémes that óthers have máde.

3 For the wícked man bóasts of his héart's desíres;
the cóvetous blasphémes and spúrns the Lórd.
4 In his príde the wícked says: 'Hé will not púnish.
There ís no Gód.' Súch are his thóughts.

5 His páth is éver untróubled;   [II 48]
your júdgment is fár from his mínd.
His énemies he regárds with contémpt.
6 He thínks: 'Néver shall I fálter:
misfórtune shall néver be my lót.'   [repeat D]

7 His móuth is full of cúrsing, guile, oppréssion,
míschief and decéit under his tóngue.
8 He líes in wáit among the réeds;
the ínnocent he múrders in sécret.

His éyes are on the wátch for the hélpless mán. [III 49]
9 He lúrks in híding like a líon in his láir;
he lúrks in híding to séize the póor;
he séizes the póor man and drágs him awáy.

10 He cróuches, prepáring to spríng,   [II 48]
and the hélpless fáll beneath his stréngth.
11 He thínks in his héart: 'God forgéts,
he hides his fáce, he dóes not sée.'

12 Aríse then, Lórd, líft up your hánd!   [III 49]
O Gód, dó not forgét the póor!
13 Whý should the wícked spúrn the Lórd
and thínk in his héart: 'Hé will not púnish'?

14 But yóu have seen the tróuble and sórrow, [II 48]
you nóte it, you táke it in hánd.
The hélpless trústs himself to yóu;
for yóu are the hélper of the órphan.

15 Bréak the pówer of the wícked and the sínner! [III 49]
Púnish his wíckedness till nóthing remáins!
16 The Lórd is kíng for éver and éver.
The héathen shall pérish from the lánd he rúles.

17 Lórd, you héar the práyer of the póor;
    you stréngthen their héarts; you túrn your éar
18 to protéct the ríghts of the órphan and oppréssed:
    so that mórtal mán may strike térror no móre.

10

The security of God's friends:
a psalm of confidence

*Another, and a picturesque variation of the theme of trust in God. The
hunters are out again, but the psalmist is already away to the refuge he
knows so well, every cranny of it, the mountain which is God. What else
can he do when all the rest has collapsed that seemed dependable? Perhaps
the attitude is as grudging as Peter's 'To whom shall we go?', or as the
Prodigal's mean motive for a return to his father, or as that of Israel, the
ungrateful wife, in Ezekiel who goes back to her husband because her
lovers do not want her any more. Doubtless our own motives are never
unmixed: something creative has disappointed us and we turn to the
Creator. Strangely enough he seems to be satisfied with this: he runs to
us, undignified like the Prodigal's father. Shall we ever understand how
humble God's love is? Even the form of a servant was not enough unless
it hung on a cross.*

FORMULA II 51

1 In the Lórd I have táken my réfuge.
    Hów can you sáy to my sóul:
    'Flý like a bírd to its móuntain.

2 See the wícked brácing their bów;
    they are fíxing their árrows on the stríng
    to shóot upright mén in the dárk.
3 Foundátions once destróyed, what can the júst do?'

4 The Lórd is in his hóly témple,
    the Lórd, whose thróne is in héaven.
    His éyes look dówn on the wórld;
    his gáze tests mórtal mén.

30

5 The Lórd tests the júst and the wícked:
the lóver of víolence he hátes.
6 He sends fíre and brímstone on the wícked;
he sends a scórching wínd as their lót.

7 The Lórd is júst and loves jústice:
the úpright shall sée his fáce.
[*Doxology*]

I I

Truth in a world of lies

*The 'truth' of God is not so much a light to the mind as a sure guide
along the uncertain way of life: 'Your commands are a light to my
feet'. Similarly, the falsehood of men which the psalmist complains of is
rather their unreliability than their tendency to lie. Hollow boasting can
persuade the less thoughtful that a quagmire is solid ground, and the
psalmists frequently denounce it: they find solidity only in God. From
him there are no high sounding promises without fulfilment: Israel's past
proves it and her future will confirm it. The psalm seems to be a liturgy:
a lament is answered by the divine promise of help pronounced by the priest:
God will arise and save; the people reply with a profession of trust.*

FORMULA III 49

2 Hélp, O Lórd, for góod men have vánished:
trúth has góne from the sóns of mén.
3 Fálsehood they spéak óne to anóther,
with lýing líps, with a fálse héart.

4 May the Lórd destróy all lýing líps,
the tóngue that spéaks hígh-sounding wórds,
5 thóse who sáy: 'Our tóngue is our stréngth;
our líps are our ówn, whó is our máster?'

6 'For the póor who are oppréssed and the néedy who
gróan
Í mysélf will aríse,' says the Lórd.
'I will gránt them the salvátion for whích they thírst.'

7 The wórds of the Lórd are wórds without álloy, [ɑ+ᴅ]
sílver from the fúrnace, séven times refíned.

8 It is yóu, O Lórd, who will táke us in your cáre
and protéct us for éver from thís generátion.

9 Sée how the wícked prówl on every síde,
while the wórthless are prized híghly by the sóns of
mén.

I2

Prayer of a man in anxiety

*The friends of God are able to take liberties, it seems; indeed, they can
be peremptory to the point of rudeness. One may suppose that they see less
danger in presumption than in despair, and no doubt they are right. Moreover, there is an undertone in this psalm that we hear elsewhere: that the
defeat of God's friend is a reflection on God himself, and with such pious
cunning, we may hope, God is content. In fact, the death and resurrection
of Christ who bore our sins is God's admission that the triumph of sin
would have affronted his own honour. And so we pray to God to safeguard
his own honour in ourselves who seem to be the custodians of it, and yet
only from God himself have the strength to guard it. This was not the
psalm that Jesus began on the cross, but it might equally well have been.
Unlike his enemies ours are inside us; we crucify ourselves; but he will
allow us to transpose this psalm into our own minor key.*

FORMULA VI 25

2 How lóng, O Lórd, will yóu forgét me?
How lóng wíll you híde your fáce?
3 How lóng must Í bear gríef in my sóul,
this sórrow in my héart dáy and níght?
How lóng shám my énemy preváil?

4 Lóok at me, ánswer me, Lórd my Gód!
Give líght to my éyes lest I fáll asleep in déath,
5 lest my énemy sáy: 'Í have overcóme him';
lest my fóes rejóice to sée my fáll.

6 As for mé, I trúst in your mérciful lóve.
   Let my héart rejoíce in your sáving hélp:
7 Let me síng to the Lórd for his góodness to mé,
   singing psálms to the náme of the Lórd, the Most Hígh.

I3

The fools

The 'fool' in the Bible is not an ignoramus; nor is he a theoretical atheist or agnostic, a phenomenon apparently unknown to the Old Testament writers living in a polytheistic world. He is one who has his values all wrong and is encouraged by past experience to behave as if God would never take action. The world, mourns the psalmist, is full of men like this. But their time will come: God will save his people from them whether they are traitors to Israel or enemies from outside. We for our part should never count ourselves exempt from Scriptural denunciations. How often, for example, have we thought 'I thank God I am not as this Pharisee'? No, we are 'foolish' too: the traitor inside us establishes his own convenient hierarchy of values. In this psalm, as in so many others, we pray God to destroy what is worst in our own selves.

FORMULA I 54

1 The fóol has sáid in his héart:
   'There is no Gód abóve.'
   Their déeds are corrúpt, deprávéd;
   not a góod man is léft.

2 From héaven the Lórd looks dówn
   on the sóns of mén
   to sée if ány are wíse,
   if ány seek Gód.

3 Áll have léft the right páth,
   depráved, every óne:
   there is nót a góod man léft,
   nó, not even óne.

4 Will the évil-doers nót understánd?
They éat up my péople
as thoúgh they were éating bréad:
they never práy to the Lórd.

5 Sée how they trémble with féar
without cáuse for féar:
for Gód is with the júst.   [repeat B]
6 You may móck the póor man's hópe,
but his réfuge is the Lórd.

7 O that Ísrael's salvátion might cóme from Zíon! [III 49]
When the Lórd delívers his péople from bóndage,
then Jácob will be glád and Ísrael rejóice.

See psalm 52

14

Moral code of a good man

*'Who goes there?' In this psalm there is a challenge for those who would
enter the presence of God. The passport is a blameless life, righteousness,
sincerity. All these are interpreted and further defined in relation to fellow-
men, because the Israelite has a strong sense of community. In the final
scrutiny before we enter the Presence the emphasis is of the same kind
(Mt. 25: 31) but given an even stronger motive—the love of Christ: 'As
often as you did it for the least of my brothers you did it for me.' If our
conscience turns to almsgiving our commonsense may object (since the wish
is father to the thought) that all this is taken care of by the State. Perhaps.
But there is much to do that lies outside this narrow field: there is the
kindness of the tongue and practical sympathy of so many kinds.*

FORMULA II 51
1 Lord, whó shall be admítted to your tént   [A+D]
and dwéll on your hóly móuntain?

2 Hé who wálks without fáult;
hé who ácts with jústice
and spéaks the trúth from his héart;
3 hé who does not slánder with his tóngue;

34

hé who does no wróng to his bróther,
who cásts no slúr on his néighbour,
4 who hólds the gódless in disdáin,
but hónours those who féar the Lórd;

hé who keeps his plédge, come what máy;
5 who tákes no ínterest on a lóan
and accépts no bríbes against the ínnocent.
Such a mán will stand fírm for éver.

15

True happiness:
a psalm of confidence

*So much lip-service is paid to the one God and so much activity to the
gods we make for ourselves. Only thoughtful experience can show how
hollow these are: the offerings we make them pay no return but a frenzy
to offer more. But perhaps this experience is necessary for most: it may
not lead to the high mysticism of the psalmist, but if we learn to turn away
and look for a while towards the more lasting Good we may find it more
satisfying after all: appetite may grow from what it feeds on. There is
even a presentiment in this psalm that such a union with God will prove
stronger than death, and in Christ it did. The risen Lord, so closely united
with his Father, descended to the place of death and came out freely,
ascending with his spoils. Nor can Death resist his Body which is the
Church: he promised that the gates of death would not withstand it.
Death, 'the last enemy', is destroyed: the resurrection of our bodies is
guaranteed by the resurrection of Christ.*

FORMULA VI 25

1 Presérve me, Gód, I take réfuge in yóu.   [A+B+F]
2 I sáy to the Lórd: 'Yóu are my Gód.
My háppiness líes in yóu alóne.'

3 He has pút into my héart a márvellous lóve   [omit c]
for the fáithful ónes who dwéll in his lánd.
4 Those who chóose other góds incréase their sórrows.
Néver will I óffer their ófferings of blóod.
Néver will I táke their náme upon my líps.

5 O Lórd, it is yóu who are my pórtion and cúp; [omit

it is yóu yoursélf who áre my príze. B+C]

6 The lót marked óut for me is mý delíght:

welcome indéed the héritage that fálls to mé!

7 I will bléss the Lórd who gíves me cóunsel,

who éven at níght dirécts my héart.

8 I kéep the Lórd ever ín my síght:

since hé is at my ríght hand, Í shall stand fírm.

9 And so my héart rejóices, my sóul is glád;

éven my bódy shall rést in sáfety.

10 For yóu will not léave my sóul among the déad,

nor lét your belóved knów decáy.

11 You will shów me the páth of lífe, [II 24 omit B]

the fúllness of jóy in your présence,

at your ríght hand háppiness for éver.

16

Appeal of an upright man

God is appealed to as a Judge. Few would dare to do this but the psalmist is sure of his worthiness. This assurance would be arrogant if there were no salutary self-mistrust—but there is. Indeed, it is a constant source of surprise for those who think of Judaism as a 'religion of works', to find how often the responsibility is thrown on God. From the earliest days this responsibility has been perceived on a national scale: only God could restore the fortunes of this people. But in this individual lament, as in so many others, God is asked to do all the work, not this time for the nation but for the lonely psalmist. We are very near to the true conception of what we call 'grace', to the idea of a God without whom we can do nothing and in whose strength we can do everything.

FORMULA IV 14

1 Lórd, hear a cáuse that is júst,

pay héed to my crý.

Túrn your éar to my práyer:

no decéit is on my líps.

2 From yóu may my júdgment come fórth.
Your éyes discern the trúth.

3 You séarch my héart, you vísit me by níght. [ɪɪɪ 12]
You tést me and you fínd in mé no wróng.
My wórds are not sínful *4* as are mén's wórds.

I képt from víolence becáuse of your wórd,
5 I képt my féet fírmly in your páths;
there wás no fáltering ín my stéps.

6 I am hére and I cáll, you will héar me, O Gód.
Túrn your éar to me; héar my wórds.
7 Displáy your great lóve, yóu whose ríght hand savés
your friénds from thóse who rebél agáinst them.

8 Guárd me as the ápple of your éye. [ɪɪ 10]
Híde me in the shádow of your wíngs
9 from the víolent attáck of the wícked.

My fóes encírcle me with déadly inténtt. [ɪɪɪ 12]
10 Their héarts tight shút, their móuths speak próudly.
11 They advánce agáinst me, and nów they surróund me.

Their éyes are wátching to stríke me to the gróund
12 as thóugh they were líons réady to cláw
or líke some young líon cróuched in híding.

13 Lord, aríse, confrónt them, stríke them dówn!
Let your swórd réscue my soúl from the wícked;
14 let your hánd, O Lórd, réscue me from mén,
from mén whose rewárd is in this présent lífe.

You gíve them their fíll of your tréasures; [ɪɪ 10]
they rejóice in abúndance of óffspring
and léave their wéalth to their chíldren.

15 As for mé, in my jústice I shall sée your fáce [ɪɪɪ 12]
and be fílled, when I awáke, with the síght of your
glóry.
[*Doxology*]

17

David's gratitude for victory

Here, as in Psalm 8, a picture of God as the great master of creation appears side by side with that of God as the jealous guardian of his servant man—here, of David who was king enough to serve the King of kings. For once we have no difficulty in identifying the 'enemies': the stormy history of David is well known to us. But the historical situation will not help: again we have to take the words to ourselves, and the 'enemies' we pray against have intangible arrows: we need the shield of God and all the warlike but spiritual apparatus that St. Paul asks for: 'the shield of faith, and the sword of the Spirit which is the word of God' (Eph. 6:16f).

FORMULA V 17

2 I lóve you, Lórd, my stréngth,
3 my róck, my fórtress, my sáviour.
My Gód is the róck where I take réfuge;
my shíeld, my mighty hélp, my strónghold.
4 The Lórd is wórthy of all práise:
when I cáll I am sáved from my fóes.

5 The wáves of déath rose abóut me;
the tórrents of destrúction assáiled me;
6 the snáres of the gráve entángled me;
the tráps of déath confrónted me.

7 In my ánguish I cálled to the Lórd;
I críed to my Gód for hélp.
From his témple he héard my vóice;
my crý cáme to his éars.

8 Then the éarth réeled and rócked;
the móuntains were sháken to their báse:
they réeled at his térrible ánger.
9 Smóke came fórth from his nóstrils
and scórching fíre from his móuth:
cóals were set abláze by its héat.

10 He lówered the héavens and came dówn,
a bláck cloud únder his féet.
11 He cáme enthróned on the chérubim,
he fléw on the wíngs of the wínd.

12 He máde the dárkness his cóvering,
the dark wáters of the clóuds, his tént.
13 A bríghtness shóne out befóre him
with háilstones and fláshes of fíre.

14 The Lórd thúndered in the héavens;
the Most Hígh let his vóice be héard.
15 He shot his árrows, scáttered the fóe,
flashed his líghtnings, and pút them to flíght.

16 The béd of the ócean was revéaled;
the foundátions of the wórld were laid báre
at the thúnder of your thréat, O Lórd,
at the blást of the bréath of your ánger.

17 From on hígh he réached down and séized me;
he drew me fórth from the míghty wáters.
18 He snátched me from my pówerful fóe,
from my énemies whose stréngth I could not mátch.

19 They assáiled me in the dáy of my misfórtune,
but the Lórd was mý suppórt.
20 He bróught me fórth into fréedom,
he sáved me becáuse he lóved me.

21 He rewárded me becáuse I was júst,
repáid me, for my hánds were cléan,
22 for I have képt the wáy of the Lórd
and have not fállen awáy from my Gód.

23 For his júdgments are áll befóre me:
I have néver neglécted his commánds.
24 I have álways been úpright befóre him;
I have képt mysélf from gúilt.

25 He repáid me becáuse I was júst
and my hánds were cléan in his éyes.
26 You are lóving with thóse who lóve you:
you shów yourself pérfect with the pérfect.

27 With the sincére you shów yourself sincére,
but the cúnning you outdó in cúnning.
28 For you sáve a húmble péople
but húmble the éyes that are próud.

29 Yóu, O Lórd, are my lámp,
my Gód who líghtens my dárkness.
30 With yóu I can bréak through any bárrier,
with my Gód I can scále any wáll.

31 As for Gód, his wáys are pérfect;
the wórd of the Lórd, purest góld.
Hé indéed is the shíeld
of áll who máke him their réfuge.

32 For whó is Gód but the Lórd?
Whó is a róck but our Gód?
33 The Gód who gírds me with stréngth
and mákes the páth safe befóre me.

34 My féet you made swíft as the déer's;
you have máde me stand fírm on the héights.
35 You have tráined my hánds for báttle
and my árms to bend the héavy bów.

36 You gáve me your sáving shíeld;
you uphéld me, tráined me with cáre.
37 You gáve me fréedom for my stéps;
my feét have néver slípped.

38 I pursúed and overtóok my fóes,
néver turning báck till they were sláin.
39 I smóte them so they cóuld not ríse;
they féll benéath my féet.

40

40 You gírded me with stréngth for báttle;
   you made my énemies fáll benéath me,
41 you máde my fóes take flíght;
   those who háted me Í destróyed.

42 They críed, but there was nó one to sáve them;
   they críed to the Lórd, but in váin.
43 I crúshed them fine as dúst before the wínd;
   trod them dówn like dírt in the stréets.

44 You sáved me from the féuds of the péople
   and pút me at the héad of the nátions.
   Péople unknówn to me sérved me:
45 when they héard of mé they obéyed me.

   Foreign nátions cáme to me crínging: [omit B]
46 foreign nátions fáded awáy.
   They came trémbling oút of their stróngholds.

47 Long lífe to the Lórd, my róck!
   Práised be the Gód who sáves me,
48 the Gód who gíves me redréss
   and subdúes péople únder me.

49 You sáved me from my fúrious fóes.
   You sét me abóve my assáilants.
   You sáved me from víolent mén,
50 so I will práise you, Lórd, among the nátions:
   I will síng a psálm to your náme.

51 He has gíven great víctories to his kíng
   and shówn his lóve for his anóinted,
   for Dávid and his sóns for éver.

18

Praise of God, creator and law-giver

The abrupt change in rhythm in the middle of a psalm together with the apparent change of subject perhaps means that we have two psalms in one. Whether this is true or not, it still remains to see what the two parts have in common, and in fact, the theme of each is the word of God. There is nature's message of God's beauty which is no less audible for being inarticulate and then, for Israel, the message of his specific will which the Law contains. For both of these we must show admiration and respect. When nature seems to us harsh and law constricting, faith must carry us through; when this is the case for others charity must work in us to help or sympathise.

FORMULA PS 30

2 The héavens procláim the glóry of Gód
  and the fírmament shows fórth the wórk of his hánds.
3 Dáy unto dáy tákes up the stóry
  and níght unto níght makes knówn the méssage.

4 No spéech, no wórd, no vóice is héard
5 yet their spán exténds through áll the eárth,
  their wórds to the útmost bóunds of the wórld.

Thére he has pláced a tént for the sún;
6 it comes fórth like a brídegroom cóming from his tént,
  rejóices like a chámpion to rún its cóurse.

7 At the énd of the ský is the rísing of the sún;
  to the fúrthest énd of the ský is its cóurse.
  There is nóthing concéaled from its búrning héat.

*   ☙   *

8 The láw of the Lórd is pérfect,   [1 52]
  it revíves the sóul.
  The rúle of the Lórd is to be trústed,
  it gives wísdom to the símple.

9 The précepts of the Lórd are ríght,
they gládden the héart.
The commánd of the Lórd is cléar,
it gives líght to the éyes.

10 The féar of the Lórd is hóly,
abíding for éver.
The decrées of the Lórd are trúth
and áll of them júst.

11 They are móre to be desíred than góld,
than the púrest of góld
and swéeter are théy than hóney,
than hóney from the cómb.

12 So in thém your sérvant finds instrúction;
great rewárd is in their kéeping.
13 But whó can detéct all his érrors?
From hídden faults acquít me.

14 From presúmption restráin your sérvant
and lét it not rúle me.
Thén shall Í be blámeless,
cléan from grave sín.

15 May the spóken wórds of my móuth,
the thóughts of my héart,
win fávour in your síght, O Lórd,
my réscuer, my róck!

19

Prayer for a king before battle

*We cannot be expected to work up an enthusiasm for some dead king's
campaign. 'Send him victorious' for only one, and his crown was made
of thorns. If we do not accept this shift of key, the psalm is unsingable
for us. This is as it should be. The word of God must always be effective
but sometimes it has done its work already in one quarter and must turn*

43

to face another situation. This is not always possible (for example, the detailed instructions for the Tabernacle in the Book of Exodus are of no further use to us), but it is possible here because we are still a monarchy: and the king is Christ.

2 May the Lord ánswer in tíme of tríal;
   may the náme of Jacob's Gód protéct you.

3 May he sénd you hélp from his shríne
   and gíve you suppórt from Zíon.
4 May he remémber áll your ófferings
   and recéive your sácrifice with fávour.

5 May he gíve you your héart's desíre
   and fulfíl every óne of your pláns.
6 May we ríng out our jóy at your víctory
   and rejóice in the náme of our Gód.
   [May the Lórd gránt all your práyers.]

7 I am súre nów that the Lórd
   will give víctory tó his anóinted,
   will replý from his hóly héaven
   with the míghty víctory of his hánd.

8 Sóme trust in cháriots or hórses,
   but wé in the náme of the Lórd.
9 Théy will collápse and fáll,
   but wé shall hóld and stand fírm.

10 Give víctory to the kíng, O Lórd,
   give ánswer on the dáy we cáll.
   [*Doxology*]

20

After victory

Another royal psalm requiring the same transposition as its predecessor. But now the victory is won and we think of the ascended Christ in his immortal and glorified body. But the war is not over yet: the spoils have to be safely gathered in. Christ has not retired to enjoy his triumph. He

*sits at the right hand of God, but God is everywhere; and so Christ is
still Emmanuel, still God with us, much more with us because the restrictions
of space and time have been taken from his body. This indeed is what the
Ascension means: not a going but a more powerful coming, not a with-
drawal but an active presence. For all this, our psalm is a Te Deum.*

2 O Lórd, your stréngth gives jóy to the kíng;
   hów your sáving hélp makes him glád!
3 You have gránted hím his héart's desíre;
   you háve not refúsed the práyer of his líps.

4 You cáme to méet him with the bléssings of succéss,
   you have sét on his héad a crówn of pure góld.
5 He ásked you for lífe and thís you have gíven,
   dáys that will lást from áge to áge.

6 Your sáving hélp has gíven him glóry.
   You have láid upón him májesty and spléndour,
7 you have gránted your bléssings to hím for éver.
   You have máde him rejóice with the jóy of your
   présence.

8 The kíng has pút his trúst in the Lórd:
   through the mércy of the Most Hígh hé shall stand
   fírm.
9 His hánd will séek and fínd all his fóes,
   his ríght hand fínd out thóse that háte him.

10 You will búrn them like a blázing fúrnace   [II 24]
   on the dáy when yóu appéar.
   And the Lórd shall destróy them in his ánger;
   fíre will swállow them úp.

11 You will wípe out their ráce from the éarth
   and their chíldren from the sóns of mén.
12 Though they plán évil agáinst you,
   though they plót, they sháll not preváil.

13 For yóu will fórce them to retréat;
   at thém you will áim with your bów.
14 O Lórd, aríse in your stréngth;
   we shall síng and práise your pówer.

45

21

The suffering servant wins the deliverance of the nations

When a dying man has the strength to whisper 'Our Father', we may suppose that his thoughts go on with the prayer his lips cannot finish. When the crucified Christ shouted the first dreadful line of this psalm his mind must have gone on to its triumphal end, thanking his Father that this dark way of desertion led to the light beyond it. But Christ does not suffer alone, nor is he glorified alone. We are 'in Christ' for better or worse, for suffering and for joy. The feeling of desertion and the uncertainty that so oddly comes with physical pain, or even with continued weakness, must be lived through in faith—faith that gives no light but only strength to go on doing what we know we must.

FORMULA III 26

2 My Gód, my Gód, whý have you forsáken me?
   You are fár from my pléa and the crý of my distréss.
3 O my Gód, I call by dáy and you gíve no replý;
   I cáll by níght and I fínd no péace.

4 Yet yóu, O Gód, are hóly,   [v 23]
   enthróned on the práises of Ísrael.
5 In yóu our fáthers put their trúst;
   they trústed and you sét them frée.
6 When they críed to yóu, they escáped.
   In you they trústed and néver in váin.

7 But Í am a wórm and no mán,
   the butt of mén, laughing-stóck of the péople.
8 Áll who sée me deríde me.
   They curl their líps, they tóss their héads.
9 'He trústed in the Lórd, let him sáve him;
   let him reléase him if thís is his fríend.'

10 Yes, it was yóu who tóok me from the wómb,
    entrústed me to my móther's bréast.
11 To yóu I was commítted from my bírth,
    from my móther's womb yóu have been my Gód.

12 Do not léave me alóne in my distréss;
come clóse, there is nóne else to hélp.

13 Mány búlls have surróunded me,
fierce búlls of Báshan close me ín.
14 Agáinst me they ópen wide their jáws,
like líons, rénding and róaring.

15 Like wáter Í am poured óut,
disjóinted are áll my bónes.
My héart has becóme like wáx,
it is mélted withín my bréast.

16 Párched as burnt cláy is my thróat,
my tóngue cléaves to my jáws.

17 Mány dógs have surróunded me,
a bánd of the wícked besét me.
They tear hóles in my hánds and my féet
16c and láy me in the dúst of déath.

18 I can cóunt every óne of my bónes.
These péople stáre at me and glóat;
19 they divíde my clóthing amóng them.
They cást lóts for my róbe.

20 O Lórd, do not léave me alóne,
my stréngth, make háste to hélp me!
21 Réscue my sóul from the swórd,
my life from the gríp of these dógs.
22 Save my life from the jáws of these líons,
my poor sóul from the hórns of these óxen.

23 I will téll of your náme to my bréthren
and práise you where théy are assémbled.
24 'You who féar the Lórd give him práise;
all sóns of Jácob, give him glóry.
Revére him, Ísrael's sóns.

25 For hé has néver despísed
nor scórned the póverty of the póor.
From hím he has not hídden his fáce,
but he héard the póor man when he críed.'

47

26 Yóu are my práise in the gréat assémbly.   [vi 25]
My vóws I will páy before thóse who féar him.
27 The póor shall éat and shall háve their fíll.
They shall práise the Lórd, thóse who séek him.
May their héarts líve for éver and éver!

28 All the éarth shall remémber and retúrn to the Lórd,
all fámilies of the nátions wórship befóre him
29 for the kíngdom is the Lórd's; he is rúler of the nátions.
30 They shall wórship him, áll the míghty of the éarth;
befóre him shall bów all who go dówn to the dúst.

And my sóul shall live for hím, *31* my chíldren sérve
him.
They shall téll of the Lórd to generátions yet to cóme,
32 decláre his fáithfulness to péoples yet unbórn:
'Thése things the Lórd has dóne.'

22

God, shepherd and host:
a psalm of confidence

*The 'rod of iron' of Psalm 2 is now a shepherd's crook, for God who
rules us lovingly keeps us also. The trust of the psalmist is so complete
that one might think the New Testament had nothing to add. But in the
course of years the Shepherd-Lord took flesh and died for his sheep—thus
he led the way through a dark valley to pastures beyond. We follow
without fear. And if we should falter, he takes us home in his arms
(Lk. 15: 5f). To such a shepherd we sing our hymn. But if, with the
psalmist, we may change our picture, he is our generous host, too. The
brimming cup he offers was dearly bought: 'Drink! This is my blood
that shall be shed.'*

FORMULA PS 24

1 The Lórd is my shépherd;
there is nóthing I shall wánt.
2 Frésh and gréen are the pástures
where he gíves me repóse.

48

near réstful wáters he léads me,
3 To revíve my drooping spírit.

He guídes me alóng the right páth;
he is trúe to his náme.
4 If I should wálk in the válley of dárkness
no évil would I féar.
You are thére with your cróok and your stáff;
with thése you give me cómfort.

5 You have prepáred a bánquet for mé
in the síght of my fóes.
My héad you have anóinted with óil;
my cúp is overflówing.

6 Surely góodness and kíndness shall fóllow me
all the dáys of my lífe.
In the Lórd's own hóuse shall I dwéll
for éver and éver.

23

*The ruler of the universe
enters his chosen dwelling place*

*'Heaven cannot contain thee', said Solomon, 'how much less this house
that I have built!' (2 Par. 6: 18). And yet the King of Glory passed
through the gates of a Temple where Israel's pilgrims 'sought his face'.
This psalm shares the astonishment of Solomon: 'Will God indeed dwell
with man on earth?' For us that wonder is surpassed. We have seen the
Son of God pass through the gate of our nature and heard him speak 'of
the temple of his body' (Jn. 2: 21). And this is not all. Mystically
assumed into that body our own selves become temples too—but we must
throw open the gates of a generous heart: 'If any man love me, my Father
will love him and we will come to him' (Jn. 14: 23). We think of this
as we sing: 'Let him enter, the King of Glory!' 'Come, Lord Jesus!'
(Apoc. 22: 20).*

FORMULA II 28

1 The Lórd's is the éarth and its fúllness,
the wórld and áll its péoples.

49

2 It is hé who sét it on the séas;
   on the wáters he máde it fírm.

3 Who shall clímb the móuntain of the Lórd?
   Who shall stánd in his hóly pláce?
4 The mán with clean hánds and pure héart,
   who desíres not wórthless thíngs,
   (who has not swórn so as to decéive his néighbour.)

5 He shall recéive bléssings from the Lórd
   and rewárd from the Gód who sáves him.
6 Súch are the mén who séek him,
   seek the fáce of the Gód of Jácob.

                    *   *   *

7 O gátes, lift hígh your héads;
   grow hígher, áncient dóors.
   Let him énter, the kíng of glóry!

8 Whó is the kíng of glóry?
   The Lórd, the míghty, the váliant,
   the Lórd, the váliant in wár.

9 O gátes, lift hígh your héads;
   grow hígher, áncient dóors.
   Let him énter, the kíng of glóry!

10 Who is hé, the kíng of glóry?
   Hé, the Lórd of ármies,
   hé is the kíng of glóry.

24

Prayer for protection and forgiveness:
an alphabetical psalm

After confident protestations of innocence, e.g. in Psalm 16, this sad admission of guilt is for us most cheering: at last we feel completely in sympathy with the psalmist, since most of us are uneasy with the saints. God is the teacher, the loving Guide: he goes in front of us and we watch him, and at times he turns round to see if we are following. This psalm is, like the Confiteor, a model 'act of contrition'. It does not try to stir up an emotional sorrow: it simply states the case, admits the guilt, and asks for mercy. Can anyone before God do more?

FORMULA V 39

1 To you, O Lórd, I líft up my sóul.
2 I trúst you, let me nót be disappóinted;
   do not lét my énemies tríumph.
3 Those who hópe in you shall nót be disappóinted,
   but only thóse who wántonly break fáith.

4 Lórd, make me knów your wáys.   [II 40]
   Lórd, téach me your páths.
5 Make me wálk in your trúth, and téach me:
   for yóu are Gód my sáviour.

   In yóu I hópe all day lóng   [V 39]
7c becáuse of your góodness, O Lórd.
6 Remémber your mércy, Lórd,
   and the lóve you have shówn from of óld.
7 Do not remémber the síns of my yóuth.
   In your lóve remémber mé.

8 The Lórd is góod and úpright.   [II 40]
   He shows the páth to thóse who stráy,
9 He guides the húmble in the ríght páth;
   He téaches his wáy to the póor.

10 His wáys are fáithfulness and lóve
for those who kéep his cóvenant and wíll.
11 Lórd, for the sáke of your náme
forgíve my guílt; for it is gréat.

12 If ányone féars the Lórd   [v 3 9]
he will shów him the páth he should chóose.
13 His sóul shall líve in háppiness
and his chíldren shall posséss the lánd.
14 The Lord's fríendship is for thóse who revére him;
to thém he revéals his cóvenant.

15 My éyes are álways on the Lórd;   [II 40]
for he réscues my féet from the snáre.
16 Túrn to mé and have mércy
for Í am lónely and póor.

17 Relíeve the ánguish of my héart
and sét me frée from my distréss.
18 Sée my afflíction and my tóil
and táke all my síns awáy.

19 Sée how mány are my fóes;   [v 39]
how víolent their hátred for mé.
20 Presérve my lífe and réscue me.
Do not disappóint me, yóu are my réfuge.
21 May ínnocence and úprightness protéct me:
for my hópe is in yóu, O Lórd.

22 Redeem Ísrael, O Gód, from áll its distréss.

25

Prayer of a man of integrity

How can I sing this psalm? Do I really 'walk in the path of perfection'?
Surely the psalmist himself is exaggerating. Dare he challenge God's
scrutiny? Perhaps we must cheat here, and put all the tenses in the optative.
After all, the psalmist himself asked for mercy: he must feel he needs it.

We certainly do. But it may be that he is speaking rather of the privileged situation in which God has placed him. He lives in a devout community and is privileged to stand near the altar. If so, we can sing with him without insincerity. Let us treat the psalm as a thanksgiving for being where we are—in the Body of Christ which we call the Church.

1 Give júdgment for mé, O Lórd:
   for I wálk the páth of perféction.
   I trúst in the Lórd; I have not wávered.

2 Exámine me, Lórd, and trý me;
   O tést my héart and my mínd,
3 for your lóve is befóre my éyes
   and I wálk accórding to your trúth.

4 I néver take my pláce with líars
   and with hýpocrites I sháll not gó.
5 I háte the évil-doer's cómpany:
   I wíll not take my pláce with the wícked.

6 To prove my ínnocence I wásh my hánds
   and take my pláce aróund your áltar,
7 sínging a sóng of thanksgíving,
   procláiming áll your wónders.

8 O Lórd, I love the hóuse where you dwéll,   [B+D]
   the pláce where your glóry abídes.

9 Do not swéep me awáy with sínners,
   nor my lífe with blóodthirsty mén
10 in whose hánds are évil plóts,
   whose ríght hands are fílled with góld.

11 As for mé, I walk the páth of perféction.
   Redéem me and shów me your mércy.
12 My fóot stands on lével gróund:
   I will bléss the Lórd in the assémbly.

26

Triumphant trust in God

One is aware of swift changes of mood in many psalms, but it would be rash to take this alone as indicating the fusion of two or more: prayer has its own rules—or none. It is not surprising that high confidence should suddenly give way to urgent appeal: Peter jumped into the lake without a thought, but he was soon shouting 'Lord, save me'. Moreover, the confidence returns even in the second part of the psalm: our fathers and mothers must leave us in the end but our Father in heaven never. The psalmist would not have been deceived by the apparent harshness of the words of Jesus: the one who loves father and mother more than me is not worthy of me.

FORMULA I 15

1 The Lórd is my líght and my hélp;
whóm shall I féar?
The Lórd is the strónghold of my lífe;
before whóm shall I shrínk?

2 When évil-dóers draw néar
to devóur my flésh,
it is théy, my énemies and fóes,
who stúmble and fáll.

3 Though an ármy encámp agáinst me
my héart would not féar.
Though wár break óut agáinst me
even thén would I trúst.

4 There is óne thing I ásk of the Lórd,
for thís I lóng,
to líve in the hóuse of the Lórd,
all the dáys of my lífe,
to sávour the swéetness of the Lórd,
to behóld his témple.

5 For thére he keeps me sáfe in his tént
in the dáy of évil.
He hídes me in the shélter of his tént,
on a róck he sets me sáfe.

6 And nów my héad shall be ráised
above my fóes who surróund me
and I shall óffer withín his tént
a sácrifice of jóy.

I will síng and make músic for the Lórd.

7 O Lórd, hear my vóice when I cáll;
have mércy and ánswer.
8 Of yóu my héart has spóken:
'Séek his fáce.'

It is your fáce, O Lórd, that I séek;
9 híde not your fáce.
Dismíss not your sérvant in ánger;
yóu have been my hélp.

Dó not abándon or forsáke me,
O Gód my hélp!
10 Though fáther and móther forsáke me,
The Lórd will recéive me.

11 Instrúct me, Lórd, in your wáy;
on an éven path léad me.
When they líe in ámbush 12 protéct me
from my énemy's gréed.
False wítnesses ríse agáinst me,
bréathing out fúry.

13 I am súre I shall sée the Lord's góodness
in the lánd of the líving.
14 Hope in hím, hold fírm and take héart.
Hópe in the Lórd!

27

Prayer in time of danger

That the Lord will not confuse him with wicked men seems often to be the worry of the psalmist—as if God might overlook him. The fear is not without its pathos but we must not take the idea too seriously: the devout will use any trick to persuade God, who, we may be sure, understands these human ways. Jesus was once pleased to be defeated by the quick wit of a woman (Mt. 15: 26–8). We may notice, too, the identification of 'the wicked' with such hypocrites as we sometimes are ourselves: a show of politeness is not charity, one may 'smile and smile and be a villain'.

FORMULA I 6

1 To yóu, O Lórd, I cáll,
　　my róck, héar me.
　　If yóu do not héed I shall becóme
　　like thóse in the gráve.

2 Héar the vóice of my pléading
　　as I cáll for hélp,
　　as I líft up my hánds in práyer
　　to your hóly pláce.

3 Do not drág me awáy with the wícked,
　　with the évil-dóers,
　　who spéak words of péace to their néighbours
　　but with évil in their héarts.

4 Repáy them as their áctions desérve   [IV 5]
　　and the málice of their déeds.
　　Repáy them for the wórk of their hánds;
　　gíve them their desérts.
5 For they ignóre the déeds of the Lórd
　　and the wórk of his hánds.
　　(May he rúin them and néver rebúild them.)

6 Bléssed be the Lórd for he has héard
my crý, my appéal.
7 The Lórd is my stréngth and my shíeld;
in hím my heart trústs.
I was hélped, my héart rejóices
and I práise him with my sóng.

8 The Lórd is the stréngth of his péople,　　　　[п 4]
a fórtress where his anóinted find hélp.
9 Save your péople; bless Ísrael your héritage.
Be their shépherd and cárry them for éver.

28

God's power seen in the storm

Praise of the power of God displayed in storm. But the strength is of a hand as powerful to calm as it is to move—a strength man can trust. The psalmist sees his land shaken from end to end, from the bulk of the Lebanon range in the north to the southern wilds of Kadesh. He is not disturbed: the Lord sits as king above the storm and blesses his people with peace. 'The Lord's voice!' It speaks in nature, it spoke in Israel's law, it spoke through the prophets, but last and most clear it spoke through the Son—this same voice, this Word, itself took flesh. At the Birth angels echoed our psalm which begins with 'glory in the highest!' and ends with 'peace to men'. Jesus is at once the power and the peace of God. We sing this sacred song to the incarnate Word.

FORMULA II 18

1 O give the Lórd you sóns of Gód,
give the Lórd glóry and pówer;
2 give the Lórd the glóry of his náme.
Adore the Lórd in his hóly court.

3 The Lord's vóice resóunding on the wáters,
the Lórd on the imménsity of wáters;
4 the vóice of the Lórd, full of pówer,
the vóice of the Lórd, full of spléndour.

5 The Lord's vóice sháttering the cédars,
the Lord shátters the cédars of Lébanon;

57

6 he makes Lébanon léap like a cálf
and Sírion like a yóung wild-óx.

7 (The Lord's vóice fláshes flames of fíre.)

8 The Lord's vóice sháking the wílderness,
the Lord shákes the wílderness of Kádesh;
9 the Lord's voíce rénding the óak tree
and strípping the fórest báre.

3b The Gód of glóry thúnders.
10 In his témple they áll cry: 'Glóry!'
The Lórd sat enthróned over the flóod;
the Lórd sits as kíng for éver.

11 The Lórd will give stréngth to his péople,
the Lórd will bless his péople with péace.

29

Thanksgiving for recovery from sickness

*'The devil was sick, the devil a monk would be. The devil was well, the
devil a monk was he.' There is some truth in this. Good health has its
own unconscious arrogance and is even accompanied sometimes by a
deceptive feeling of holiness. Sickness opens our eyes: we look back on
our lives and are frightened by the selfishness of our motives. When we
recover, our conduct may not improve but at least we may be grateful for
our recovery in our prayers. But the real sickness is of mind and soul, and
if we ask God to cure us of this, the dawn will break. The psalmist knows
that all these sicknesses will pass, but St. Paul can add the further comfort
beyond the horizon of this psalm: in the opposite scale of the balance is
the 'eternal weight of glory'.*

FORMULAS V 30 [A+B]
VI 33 [C+D]

2 I will práise you, Lórd, yóu have réscued me
and have nót let my énemies rejóice óver me.

*   *   *

3 O Lórd, I críed to you for hélp
and yóu, my Gód, have héaled me.
4 O Lórd, you have ráised my sóul from the déad,
restóred me to lífe from those who sínk into the gráve.

5 Sing psálms to the Lórd, you who lóve him,
give thánks to his hóly náme.
6 His ánger lasts a móment; his fávour all through lífe.
At níght there are téars, but jóy comes with dáwn.

7 I sáid to mysélf in my good fórtune:
'Nóthing will éver distúrb me.'
8 Your fávour had sét me on a móuntain fástness,
then you híd your fáce and I was pút to confúsion.

9 To yóu, Lórd, I críed,
to my Gód I máde appéal:
10 'What prófit would my déath be, my góing to the
gráve?
Can dúst give you práise or procláim your trúth?'

11 The Lórd lístened and had píty.
The Lórd cáme to my hélp.
12 For mé you have chánged my móurning into dáncing,
you remóved my sáckcloth and gírded me with jóy.
13 So my sóul sings psálms to you uncéasingly.
O Lord my Gód, I will thánk you for éver.

30

Confident prayer in distress

*False accusation and violence teaches the psalmist that truth and peace can
be surely found only in God. It is the situation of Jeremiah (e.g. Jer.
20: 7ff), of the author of the very similar Psalm 21, and of Jesus himself
who quotes that psalm and this on the Cross. There is an admission of
momentary fear, a 'Let this cup of suffering pass me by', but also a swift
recovery: it is not perhaps the perfect designation of 'Thy will be done',
but is at least a confident cry for help. This is usually as much as we can
manage ourselves, and no doubt in God's eyes it is enough. Our lives are in
his hands, the psalmist says twice: the hands of God are sure and gentle.*

2 In yóu, O Lórd, I take réfuge.
Let me néver be pút to sháme.
In your jústice, sét me frée,
3 héar me and spéedily réscue me.

Be a róck of réfuge fór me,
a míghty strónghold to sáve me,
4 for yóu are my róck, my strónghold.
For your náme's sake, léad me and gúide me.

5 Reléase me from the snáres they have hídden
for yóu are my réfuge, Lórd.
6 Into your hánds I comménd my spírit.
It is yóu who will redéem me, Lórd.

O Gód of trúth, *7* you detést
those who wórship fálse and empty góds.
8 As for mé, I trúst in the Lórd:
let me be glád and rejóice in your lóve.

Yóu who have séen my afflíction
and taken héed of my sóul's distréss,
9 have not hánded me óver to the énemy,
but sét my féet at lárge.

* * *

10 Have mércy on mé, O Lórd,   [I 14]
for Í am in distréss.
Téars have wásted my éyes,
my thróat and my héart.

11 For my lífe is spént with sórrow
and my yéars with síghs.
Afflíction has bróken down my stréngth
and my bónes waste awáy.

12 In the fáce of áll my fóes
Í am a repróach,
an óbject of scórn to my néighbours
and of féar to my fríends.

Thóse who sée me in the strée
run fár awáy from me.
13 Í am like a déad man, forgótten,
like a thíng thrown awáy.

14 I have héard the slánder of the crówd,
féar is all aróund me,
as they plót togéther agáinst me,
as they plán to take my lífe.

15 But as for mé, I trust in yóu, Lórd,
I say: 'Yóu are my Gód.
16 My lífe is in your hánds, delíver me
from the hánds of those who háte me.

17 Let your fáce shíne on your sérvant.
Sáve me in your lóve.
18 Let me nót be put to sháme for I cáll you,
let the wícked be shámed!

Lét them be sílenced in the gráve,
19 let lýing lips be dúmb,
that speak háughtily agáinst the júst
with príde and contémpt.'

*   *   *

20 How gréat is the góodness, Lórd,
that you kéep for those who féar you,
that you shów to thóse who trúst you
in the síght of mén.

21 You híde them in the shélter of your présence
from the plótting of mén:
you kéep them sáfe within your tént
from dispúting tóngues.

22 Bléssed be the Lórd who has shówn me   [omit c]
the wónders of his lóve
in a fórtified cíty.

61

23 'I am fár remóved from your síght'
I sáid in my alárm.
Yet you héard the vóice of my pléa
when I críed for hélp.

24 Lóve the Lórd, all you sáints.
He guárds his fáithful
but the Lórd will repáy to the fúll
those who áct with príde.

25 Be stróng, let your héart take cóurage,
all who hópe in the Lórd.
[*Doxology*]

3 1

The joy of being forgiven:
second psalm of repentance

*Perhaps it is unfair to call this a 'penitential' psalm—or at least the mood
is more one of joy than of penance. There may be a lesson here that the
virtuous life is not a gloomy one. Suppression and self-deception, as the
psalm admits, never made for happiness: free acknowledgement to God
and to ourselves is a duty, but it is also a health medicine. This conclusion
which the psalmist draws is followed by the voice of God confirming it:
God is anxious to lead us along this way: we have only to be docile, he
will do the rest.*

FORMULA IV 5

1 Happy the mán whose offénce is forgíven,
whose sín is remítted.
2 O háppy the mán to whom the Lórd
impútes no guílt,
in whose spírit is no guíle.

3 I kept it sécret and my fráme was wásted.
I gróaned all day lóng
4 for níght and dáy your hánd
was héavy upón me.

62

Indéed, my stréngth was dried úp
as by the súmmer's héat.

5 But nów I have acknówledged my síns;
my guílt I did not híde.
I sáid: 'Í will conféss
my offénce to the Lórd.'
And yóu, Lórd, have forgíven
the guílt of my sín.

6 So let évery good mán pray to yóu
in the tíme of néed.
The flóods of wáter may reach hígh
but hím they shall not réach.
7 Yóu are my híding place, O Lórd;
you sáve me from distréss.
(You surróund me with críes of delíverance.)

*   *   *

8 Í will instrúct you and téach you
the wáy you should gó;
Í will gíve you cóunsel
with my éye upón you.

9 Be not like hórse and múle, unintélligent,
needing brídle and bít,
élse they wíll not appróach you.
10 Many sórrows has the wícked
but hé who trústs in the Lórd,
loving mércy surróunds him.

*   *   *

11 Rejóice, rejóice in the Lórd,
exúlt, you júst!
O cóme, ríng out your jóy,
all you úpright of héart.

32

Joyful song to the Creator: national hymn of thanksgiving

Perhaps from fear of emotionalism, clamorous joy seems to be suspect in religion. And yet God gave us the power to shout no less than to whisper. One feels that the Hebrew at least appreciated this. After all, the cosmos is his, and the nations on this planet, and the chosen people, and most of all those who revere him. Because his strength is infinite, the width of its range does not hinder the depth of its penetration. Indeed, the individual person feels all the more secure when he knows that all creation can be arranged effortlessly for his own ultimate happiness. It would be unnatural if such a faith did not produce a joy that expresses itself humbly and yet triumphantly.

FORMULA II 18

1 Ring out your jóy to the Lórd, O you júst;
for praise is fítting for lóyal héarts.

2 Give thánks to the Lórd upon the hárp,
with a tén-stringed lúte sing him sóngs.
3 O síng him a sóng that is néw,
play lóudly, with áll your skíll.

4 For the wórd of the Lórd is fáithful
and áll his wórks to be trústed.
5 The Lórd loves jústice and ríght
and fílls the éarth with his lóve.

6 By his wórd the héavens were máde,
by the bréath of his móuth all the stárs.
7 He collécts the wáves of the ócean;
he stóres up the dépths of the séa.

8 Let all the éarth féar the Lórd,
all who líve in the wórld revére him.
9 He spóke; and it cáme to bé.
He commánded; it spráng into béing.

64

10 He frustrátes the desígns of the nátions,
   he deféats the pláns of the péoples.
11 His ówn designs shall stánd for éver,
   the pláns of his héart from age to áge.

12 They are háppy, whose Gód is the Lórd,
   the péople he has chósen as his ówn.
13 From the héavens the Lórd looks fórth,
   he sées all the chíldren of mén.

14 From the pláce where he dwélls he gázes
   on áll the dwéllers on the éarth,
15 he who shápes the héarts of them áll
   and consíders áll their déeds.

16 A kíng is not sáved by his ármy,
   nor a wárrior presérved by his stréngth.
17 A váin hope for sáfety is the hórse;
   despíte its pówer it cannot sáve.

18 The Lórd looks on thóse who revére him,
   on thóse who hópe in his lóve,
19 to réscue their sóuls from déath,
   to kéep them alíve in fámine.

20 Our sóul is wáiting for the Lórd.
   The Lórd is our hélp and our shíeld.
21 In hím do our héarts find jóy.
   We trúst in his hóly náme.

22 May your lóve be upón us, O Lórd,
   as we pláce all our hópe in yóu.
   [Doxology]

33

Praise and fear of God:
an alphabetical psalm

'Look towards him and be radiant.' John Fisher recited this line when he saw that the sun shone behind the scaffold. This is a song for martyrs: the Lord sets them free from all their terrors. But it is also a song for the small martyrdoms of every day whether volunteered or simply accepted. One may be discouraged by one's failure in past trials, weakness in those of the present, uncertainty of one's resistance in the future: but of course our own weapons are always rusting and loose in our hands, the bright and effective sword is in the hand of God alone. There will be no ultimate defeat, not a bone broken for those who are one with the Lamb of our Passover on the Cross.

FORMULA II 53

2 I will bléss the Lórd at all tímes,
   his práise álways on my líps;
3 in the Lórd my sóul shall make its bóast.
   The húmble shall héar and be glád.

4 Glórify the Lórd with mé.
   Togéther let us práise his náme.
5 I sóught the Lórd and he ánswered me;
   from all my térrors he sét me frée.

6 Lóok towards hím and be rádiant;
   let your fáces nót be abáshed.
7 This póor man cálled; the Lord héard him
   and réscued him from áll his distréss.

8 The ángel of the Lórd is encámped
   around thóse who revére him, to réscue them.
9 Taste and sée that the Lórd is góod.
   He is háppy who seeks réfuge in hím.

10 Revére the Lórd, you his sáints.
   They lack nóthing, thóse who revére him.
11 Strong líons suffer wánt and go húngry
   but thóse who seek the Lórd lack no bléssing.

12 Cóme, chíldren, and héar me
that I may téach you the féar of the Lórd.
13 Who is hé who lóngs for lífe
and many dáys, to enjóy his prospérity?

14 Then kéep your tóngue from évil
and your líps from spéaking decéit.
15 Turn asíde from évil and do góod;
séek and stríve after péace.

16 The Lórd turns his fáce against the wícked
to destróy their remémbrance from the éarth.
17 The Lórd turns his éyes to the júst
and his éars to théir appéal.

18 They cáll and the Lórd héars
and réscues them in áll their distréss.
19 The Lord is clóse to the bróken-héarted;
those whose spírit is crúshed he will sáve.

20 Mány are the tríals of the júst man
but ′from them áll the Lórd will réscue him.
21 He will keep guárd over áll his bónes,
not óne of his bónes shall be bróken.

22 Évil brings déath to the wícked;
those who háte the góod are dóomed.
23 The Lord ránsoms the sóuls of his sérvants.
Those who híde in him shall nót be condémned.

34

Appeal for vindication

*The psalmists are not frightened to mix their metaphors freely, and as a
result our many-sided God appears in his solid dimension. Here he is first
a soldier, then a farmer on his threshing-floor (because God's 'angel' is
God himself), then a poacher using the net that others have left, last of all
and less graphically a counsel for the defence ready to cross-examine and*

to tear false witnesses to pieces. The witness against us is Satan (*'the adversary'*) *as he was against Job (Jb. 1: 6-11): but the counsel for the defence is the Spirit (Rom. 8: 26f). Can we fear the verdict? The arguments of the prosecuting counsel are strong, but they reckon without the mercy of the judge.*

1 O Lórd, plead my cáuse against my fóes;
  fight thóse who fight mé.
2 Táke up your búckler and shíeld;
  aríse to hélp me.

3 Táke up the jávelin and the spéar
  against thóse who pursúe me.
  O Lórd, sáy to my sóul:
  'Í am your salvátion.'

4 Let thóse who séek my lífe
  be shámed and disgráced.
  Let thóse who plan évil agáinst me
  be róuted in confúsion.

5 Let them bé like cháff before the wínd;
  let God's ángel scátter them.
6 Let their páth be slíppery and dárk;
  let God's ángel pursúe them.

7 They have hídden a nét for me wántonly;   [IV 37]
  they have dúg a pít.
8 Let rúin fáll upón them
  and táke them by surpríse.
  Let them be cáught in the nét they have hídden;
  let them fáll into their pít.

9 But my sóul shall be jóyful in the Lórd
  and rejóice in his salvátion.
10 My whóle béing will sáy:
  'Lord, whó is like yóu
  who réscue the wéak from the stróng
  and the póor from the oppréssor?'

68

11 Lýing wítnesses aríse   [ɪ 37]
and accúse me unjústly.
12 They repáy me évil for góod:
my sóul is forlórn.

13 When they were síck I wént into móurning,   [ɪv 37]
afflícted with fásting.
My práyer was éver on my líps,
14 as for a bróther, a fríend.
I wént as though móurning a móther,
bówed down with gríef.

15 Now that Í am in tróuble they gáther,
they gáther and móck me.
They táke me by surpríse and stríke me
and téar me to píeces.
16 They provóke me with móckery on móckery
and gnásh their téeth.

17 O Lórd, how lóng will you look ón?
Cóme to my réscue!
Save my lífe from these ráging béasts,
my sóul from these líons.
18 I will thánk you in the gréat assémbly,
Amid the thróng I will práise you.

19 Do not lét my lýing fóes   [ɪ 37]
rejóice over mé.
Do not lét those who háte me unjústly
wink éyes at each óther.

20 They wísh no péace to the péaceful   [ɪv 37]
who líve in the lánd.
They máke decéitful plóts
21 and with móuths wide ópen
their crý agáinst me is: 'Yés!
We sáw you dó it!'

22 O Lórd, you have séen, do not be sílent,   [ɪ 37]
do not stánd afar óff!
23 Awáke, stír to my defénce,
to my cáuse, O Gód!

24 Víndicate me, Lórd, in your jústice,
do not lét them rejóice.
25 Do not lét them think: 'Yés! we have wón,
we have bróught him to an énd!'

26 Let them be shámed and bróught to disgráce
who rejóice at my misfórtune.
Let them be cóvered with sháme and confúsion
who ráise themselves agáinst me.

27 Let there be jóy for thóse who love my cáuse. [IV 37]
Let them sáy without énd:
'Gréat is the Lórd who delíghts
in the péace of his sérvant.'
28 Then my tóngue shall spéak of your jústice,
all day lóng of your práise.

35

Man's malice: God's goodness

*Surely we have two psalms here, despite the attempt of the last two verses
to bind them together? Nevertheless, the contrast of the two halves is
instructive. In the first there is a personified oracular authority—and it is
Sin: a master of willing slaves who do not dare to use their own judgment
or reflect on their own unhappiness. In the second there is another principle
more active still, tested by the happiness it gives: it is as deep as the sea
and as high as Olympus—God's love for man and beast. The first
authority is the end of all wisdom, the second the beginning of it, and in
its light we can see the jig-saw pattern of created things and insert our
own piece where it belongs. And when the pattern is invisible the love
of God must guide our hand.*

FORMULA I 54

2 Sín spéaks to the sínner
in the dépths of his héart.
There ís no féar of Gód
befóre his éyes.

3 He so flátters himsélf in his mínd
that he knóws not his guílt.
4 In his móuth are míschief and decéit.
All wísdom is góne.

5 He plóts the deféat of góodness
as he líes on his béd.
He has sét his fóot on evil wáys,
he clíngs to what is évil.

　　　　*　　*　　*

6 Your lóve, Lord, réaches to héaven;
your trúth to the skíes.
7 Your jústice is líke God's móuntain,
your júdgments like the déep.

To both mán and béast you give protéction.　　　[II 53]
O Lórd, *8* how précious is your lóve.
My Gód, the sóns of mén
find réfuge in the shélter of your wíngs.

9 They féast on the ríches of your hóuse;
they drínk from the stréam of your delíght.
10 In yóu is the sóurce of life
and ín your líght we see líght.

11 Keep on lóving thóse who knów you,
doing jústice for úpright héarts.
12 Let the fóot of the próud not crúsh me
nor the hánd of the wícked cast me óut.

13 Sée how the évil-doers fáll!
Flung dówn, they shall néver aríse.
[*Doxology*]

36

Reflections on good and evil: an alphabetical psalm

This psalm offers a very simple solution to the problem of evil which will satisfy few today and indeed did not satisfy, for example, the inspired author of the Book of Job. Nevertheless, the act of faith that prompts it is not only touching but also, if we look far enough, fully justified. If this were not true we could not recite the psalm with conviction. But once we have enlarged the perspective beyond this present life—which the psalmist has not done—we can take the psalm to ourselves. The 'little longer' that a good man has to wait for his reward may be all the rest of his life, but this is a short time when he thinks of the life to come. Beside this perception, however, there should be another, this time not so much horizontal as vertical: underneath the denunciation of 'the wicked man' he should see the condemnation of wickedness itself, in our own selves especially.

FORMULA II I

1 Do not frét becáuse of the wícked;
   do not énvy thóse who do évil:
2 for they wíther quíckly like gráss
   and fáde like the gréen of the fíelds.

3 If you trúst in the Lórd and do góod,
   then you will líve in the lánd and be secúre.
4 If you fínd your delíght in the Lórd,
   he will gránt your héart's desíre.

5 Commít your lífe to the Lórd,
   trust in hím and hé will áct,
6 so that your jústice breaks fórth like the líght,
   your cáuse like the nóon-day sún.

7 Be stíll before the Lórd and wait in pátience;
   do not frét at the mán who próspers;
   a mán who makes évil plóts
14c to bríng down the néedy and the póor.

8 Calm your ánger and forgét your ráge;
   do not frét, it ónly leads to évil.

9 For thóse who do évil shall pérish;
the pátient shall inhérit the lánd.

10 A little lónger—and the wícked shall have góne.
Lóok at his pláce, he is not thére.
11 But the húmble shall ówn the lánd
and enjóy the fúllness of péace.

12 The wícked man plóts against the júst
and gnáshes his téeth agáinst him;
13 But the Lórd láughs at the wícked
for he sées that his dáy is at hánd.

14 The swórd of the wícked is dráwn,
his bow is bént to sláughter the úpright.
15 Their swórd shall píerce their own héarts
and their bóws shall be bróken to píeces.

16 The júst man's féw posséssions
are bétter than the wícked man's wéalth;
17 for the pówer of the wícked shall be bróken
and the Lórd will suppórt the júst.

18 He protécts the líves of the úpright,
their héritage will lást for éver.
19 They shall nót be put to sháme in evil dáys,
in time of fámine their fóod shall not fáil.

20 But áll the wícked shall pérish
and áll the énemies of the Lórd.
Théy are like the béauty of the méadows,
they shall vánish, they shall vánish like smóke.

21 The wícked man bórrows withóut repáying,
but the júst man is génerous and gíves.
22 Those bléssed by the Lórd shall own the lánd,
but thóse he has cúrsed shall be destróyed.

23 The Lórd guides the stéps of a mán
and makes sáfe the páth of one he lóves.
24 Though he stúmble he shall néver fáll
for the Lórd hólds him by the hánd.

25 I was yóung and nów I am óld,
but I have néver seen the júst man forsáken
nor his chíldren bégging for bréad.   [repeat B]
26 All the dáy he is génerous and lénds
and his chíldren becóme a bléssing.

27 Then túrn away from évil and do góod
and yóu shall have a hóme for éver;
28 for the Lórd lóves jústice
and will néver forsáke his fríends.

The unjúst shall be wíped out for éver
and the chíldren of the wícked destróyed.
29 The júst shall inhérit the lánd;
thére they shall líve for éver.

30 The júst man's móuth utters wísdom
and his líps spéak what is ríght;
31 the láw of his Gód is in his héart,
his stéps shall be sáved from stúmbling.

32 The wícked man wátches for the júst
and séeks occásion to kíll him.
33 The Lórd will not léave him in his pówer
nor lét him be condémned when he is júdged.

34 Then wáit for the Lórd, keep to his wáy.
It is hé who will frée you from the wícked,
raise you úp to posséss the lánd
and sée the wícked destróyed.

35 I have séen the wícked triúmphant,
tówering like a cédar of Lébanon.
36 I pássed by agáin; he was góne.
I séarched; he was nówhere to be fóund.

37 See the júst man, márk the úpright,
for the péaceful man a fúture lies in stóre,
38 but sínners shall áll be destróyed.
No fúture lies in stóre for the wícked.

39 The salvátion of the júst comes from the Lórd,
their strónghold in tíme of distréss.
40 The Lórd hélps them and delívers them
and sáves them: for their réfuge is in hím.

37

Acknowledgment of guilt: third psalm of repentance

Unlike its predecessor this psalm needs no transference of thought. One sometimes wonders if commentators are not too quick to take terms like those used here in their strictly literal sense. Is it really some specific sickness that troubles the psalmist? Or is it perhaps the graver sickness of the heart? In any case, it is the sense of sin that oppresses, the cure can come only from the Lord. The tone of distress is strongly comforting. We so often imagine that the sacred writers of Israel were innocent and saintly, but behind these words there seems to be a consciousness of serious and repeated sin. If so, the lesson for us is all the sharper: the greater the sin, the greater must be the confidence, not of course in ourselves but in God.

FORMULA V 3

2 O Lórd, do not rebúke me in your ánger;
do not púnish me, Lórd, in your ráge.
3 Your árrows have sunk déep in mé;
your hánd has come dówn upón me.
4 Through your ánger all my bódy is síck:
through my sín, there is no héalth in my límbs.

5 My guílt towers hígher than my héad;
it is a wéight too héavy to béar.
6 My wóunds are fóul and féstering,
the resúlt of my ówn fólly.
7 I am bówed and bróught to my knées.
I go móurning áll the day lóng.

8 All my fráme búrns with féver;
áll my bódy is síck.
9 Spént and útterly crúshed,
I cry alóud in ánguish of héart.

75

10 O Lórd, you knów all my lónging:
my gróans are not hídden from yóu.
11 My heart thróbs, my stréngth is spént;
the very líght has góne from my éyes.

12 My fríends avóid me like a léper;
those clósest to me stánd afar óff.
13 Those who plót against my lífe lay snáres;
those who séek my rúin speak of hárm,
planning tréachery áll the day lóng.

14 But Í am like the déaf who cannot héar,
like the dúmb unáble to spéak.
15 I am like a mán who hears nóthing
in whose móuth is nó defénce.

16 I cóunt on yóu, O Lórd:
it is yóu, Lord Gód, who will ánswer.
17 I pray: 'Do not lét them móck me,
those who tríumph if my fóot should slíp.'

18 For Í am on the póint of fálling
and my páin is álways befóre me.
19 I conféss that Í am guílty
and my sín fílls me with dismáy.

20 My wánton énemies are númberless
and my lýing fóes are mány.
21 They repáy me évil for góod
and attáck me for séeking what is ríght.

22 O Lórd, dó not forsáke me!
My Gód, do not stáy afar óff!
23 Make háste and cóme to my hélp,
O Lórd, my Gód, my sáviour!

38

No abiding city

It has been said that the lesson of the sad book of Ecclesiastes is 'Blessed are not the rich' and that this is at least a step towards 'Blessed are the poor'. This melancholy psalm has perhaps the same virtue: it emphasises the shortness of life and the impermanence of all it offers. There is no hint of a life to come: revelation had a long way to go. All the psalmist could ask for would be a resigned acceptance of his human condition. And yet even this is a stepping-stone: his hope is in the eternal Lord who could not desert him. He is not far from realising that death without further hope would be the desertion he cannot believe in.

FORMULA V 9

2 I sáid: 'I will be wátchful of my wáys
for féar I should sín with my tóngue.
I will pút a cúrb on my líps
when the wícked man stánds befóre me.'
3 I was dúmb, sílent and stíll.
His prospérity stírred my gríef.

4 My héart was búrning withín me.
At the thóught of it, the fíre blazed úp
and my tóngue búrst into spéech:
5 'O Lórd, you have shówn me my énd,
how shórt is the léngth of my dáys.
Now I knów how fléeting is my lífe.

6 You have gíven me a shórt span of dáys;
my lífe is as nóthing in your síght.
A mere bréath, the mán who stood so fírm,
7 a mere shádow, the mán passing bý,
a mere bréath the ríches he hóards,
not knówing whó will háve them.'

8 And nów, Lord, whát is there to wáit for?
In yóu rests áll my hópe.

77

9 Set me frée from áll my síns,
do not máke me the táunt of the fóol.
10 I was sílent, not ópening my líps,
because thís was áll your dóing.

11 Take awáy your scóurge from mé.
I am crúshed by the blóws of your hánd.
12 You púnish man's síns and corréct him;
like the móth you devóur all he tréasures.
Mortal mán is no móre than a bréath;
13 O Lórd, héar my práyer.

O Lórd, turn your éar to my crý.
Dó not be déaf to my téars.
In your hóuse I am a pássing guést,
a pílgrim, like áll my fáthers.
14 Look awáy that I may bréathe agáin
befóre I depárt to be no móre.

39

Thanksgiving and further plea for help

The Epistle to the Hebrews (10: 5-7) invites us to hear verses 7-9 of this psalm as if Christ himself were speaking them. And it is true that we could recite vv. 1-11 along with him and in his name, thanking God for all that he has done. There is a quick change from thanksgiving to insistent appeal in the second half (vv. 12-18) and this part, identical with Psalm 69, was apparently a separate psalm at first. It is not improbable that the Epistle to the Hebrews has those in mind who had served as priests in the now ruined temple: in place of their sacrifices which God no longer asked for stands the free and perfect offering that is Christ himself who like Isaiah before him said 'Here am I! Send me' (Is. 6-8).

FORMULA I 42
[omit c]

2 I wáited, I wáited for the Lórd
and he stóoped down to mé;
he héard my crý.

3 He dréw me from the déadly pít,
from the míry cláy.
He sét my féet upon a róck
and made my fóotsteps fírm.

4 He pút a new sóng into my móuth,
práise of our Gód.
Mány shall sée and féar
and shall trúst in the Lórd.

5 Háppy the mán who has pláced
his trúst in the Lórd
and has nót gone óver to the rébels
who fóllow false góds.

6 How mány, O Lórd my Gód,
are the wónders and desígns
that yóu have wórked for ús;
you háve no équal.
Shóuld I procláim and spéak of them,   [repeat a+d]
they are móre than I can téll!

7 You do not ásk for sácrifice and ófferings,
but an ópen éar.
You do not ásk for hólocaust and víctim.
8 Instéad, here am Í.

In the scróll of the bóok it stands wrítten
9 that Í should do your wíll.
My Gód, I delíght in your láw
in the dépth of my héart.

10 Your jústice Í have procláimed
in the gréat assémbly.
My líps I háve not séaled;
you knów it, O Lórd.

11 I have not hídden your jústice in my héart
but decláred your faithful hélp.
I have not hídden your lóve and your trúth
from the gréat assémbly.

12 O Lórd, you wíll not withhóld
your compássion from mé.
Your mérciful lóve and your trúth
will álways guárd me.

13 For Í am besét with évils
too mány to be cóunted.
My síns have fállen upón me
and my síght fáils me.
They are móre than the háirs of my héad   [repeat
and my héart sínks.   c+d]

14 O Lórd, cóme to my réscue,
Lord, cóme to my áid.
15 O lét there be sháme and confúsion
on thóse who seek my lífe.

O lét them turn báck in confúsion,
who delíght in my hárm.
16 Let them be appálled, cóvered with sháme,
who jéer at my lót.

17 O lét there be rejóicing and gládness
for áll who séek you.
Let them éver say: 'The Lórd is gréat',
who lóve your saving hélp.

18 As for mé, wrétched and póor,
the Lórd thinks of mé.
Yóu are my réscuer, my hélp,
O Gód, do not deláy.

40

Prayer in sickness and betrayal

It is not uncommon to find the psalmist publicly thanking God for recovery from illness, and with this, it seems, the psalm begins. With v. 4 we are taken back to the distress now over. In this description we find words familiar to us from St. John's Gospel (13: 18). To reconcile the Jews to the idea of a suffering Messiah the evangelists try to show from the Old Testament how suffering was after all to be expected. If the admired prophets of Israel could be persecuted and betrayed, why not the Messiah himself? Our Lord had called Judas his friend (Mt. 26: 50) and Judas had 'eaten his bread' with him (Mt. 26: 23) but turned against him. The enemies of Jesus, like those in this psalm, thought that the name of Jesus could be forgotten (Acts 4: 18). They were wrong.

FORMULA VI 11

2 Happy the mán who consíders the póor and the wéak.
　The Lórd will sáve him in the dáy of évil,
3 will guárd him, give him lífe, make him háppy in the lánd
　and will nót give him úp to the wíll of his fóes.
4 The Lórd will hélp him on his béd of páin,
　he will bríng him báck from síckness to héalth.

5 As for mé, I said: 'Lórd, have mércy on mé,
　heal my sóul for Í have sínned agáinst you.'
6 My fóes are spéaking évil agáinst me.
　'How lóng before he díes and his náme be forgótten?'
7 They cóme to vísit me and spéak empty wórds,
　their héarts full of málice, they spréad it abróad.

8 My énemies whísper togéther agáinst me.
　They áll weigh úp the évil which is ón me:
9 'Some déadly thíng has fástened upón him,
　he will nót rise agáin from whére he líes.'
10 Thus éven my fríend, in whóm I trústed,
　who áte my bréad, has túrned agáinst me.

11 But yóu, O Lórd, have mércy on mé.
　Let me ríse once móre and Í will repáy them.
12 By thís I shall knów that yóu are my fríend,
　if my fóes do not shóut in tríumph óver me.
13 If yóu uphóld me Í shall be unhármed
　and sét in your présence for évermóre.

*　　*　　*

14 Bléssed be the Lórd, the Gód of Ísrael
　from áge to áge. Amén. Amén.

41

The exile's nostalgia for God's temple

The exiled Levite is far from Jerusalem, in the land where the Jordan rises; the sound of its falling waters is to him a dirge for the lost happiness of Temple feasts. We, too, are in exile and this psalm should deepen our consciousness of it. But our longing is not for 'this mountain or that' (Jn. 4: 21) as the psalmist's was for Zion. Our Lord has brought us a higher hope. Our destiny is to 'see the face of God', not only in the mediating forms of sacred ceremony; we are to see him 'as he is' (1 Jn. 3: 2). Ask God for the desire of heaven.

FORMULA I 29

2 Líke the déer that yéarns
for rúnning stréams,
só my sóul is yéarning
for yóu, my Gód.

3 My sóul is thírsting for Gód,
the Gód of my lífe;
whén can I énter and sée
the fáce of Gód?

4 My téars have becóme my bréad,
by níght, by dáy,
as I héar it sáid all the day lóng:
'Whére is your Gód?'

5 Thése things will Í remémber
as I póur out my sóul:
how I would léad the rejóicing crówd
into the hóuse of Gód,
amid críes of gládness and thanksgíving,
the thróng wild with jóy.

6 Whý are you cast dówn, my sóul,
why gróan withín me?
Hope in Gód; I will práise him stíll,
my sáviour and my Gód.

7 My sóul is cast dówn withín me
   as I thínk of yóu,
   from the cóuntry of Jórdan and Mount Hérmon,
   from the Híll of Mízar.

8 Déep is cálling on déep,
   in the róar of wáters:
   your tórrents and áll your wáves
   swept óver mé.

9 By dáy the Lórd will sénd
   his lóving kíndness;
   by níght I will síng to hím,
   praise the Gód of my lífe.

10 I will sáy to Gód, my róck:
   'Whý have you forgótten me?
   Whý do Í go móurning
   oppréssed by the fóe?'

11 With críes that píerce me to the héart,
   my énemies revíle me,
   sáying to me áll the day lóng:
   'Whére is your Gód?'

12 Whý are you cast dówn, my sóul,
   why gróan withín me?
   Hope in Gód; I will práise him stíll,
   my sáviour and my Gód.

42

Longing for God's dwelling place

*Psalm 41 is here continued. The exile in the dark of paganism asks for
such a pillar of fire as led his fathers home. He appeals to God's 'truth',
which means, in biblical idiom, God's staunchness to his trusting servants.
This light and this truth, two guardians of the Throne, will take the
exile by the hand to the altar of sacrifice, heart of his well-loved Temple.*

83

The priest at the foot of our altar, and we with him, stands on common ground but, unlike the psalmist, he is not dwelling upon the sinfulness around him; rather he is cast down by his own. With him we hesitate, asking God's forgiving grace to lead us to the holy mountain of his Son's sacrifice.

1 Defénd me, O Gód, and plead my cáuse
against a gódless nátion.
From decéitful and cúnning mén
réscue me, O Gód.

2 Since yóu, O Gód, are my strónghold,
whý have you rejécted me?
Whý do Í go móurning
oppréssed by the fóe?

3 O sénd forth your líght and your trúth;
let thése be my guíde.
Let them bríng me to your hóly móuntain
to the pláce where you dwéll.

4 And I will cóme to the áltar of Gód,
the Gód of my jóy.
My redéemer, I will thánk you on the hárp,
O Gód, my Gód.

5 Whý are you cast dówn, my sóul,
why gróan withín me?
Hope in Gód; I will práise him stíll,
my sáviour and my Gód.

43

God's people in time of disaster: a national lament

The problem of evil is posed here on a national plane. At this level it had been solved plausibly enough by the book of Judges: if the nation had sinned, the nation was punished. This solution had been found unsatisfactory in the case of individuals: the experience of Job and many others

*had disproved the necessary connection between sin and suffering. Here the
solution is surprisingly found defective even for the nation at large, and
the baffled psalmist can only pray. Elijah had ironically suggested to the
prophets of Baal that their god might be asleep—can Yahweh sleep as
well? But the psalmist's language has the extravagance born of urgency,
as our own might have when we think of devout Christians persecuted. It
is not our business to penetrate the mystery; it is our business to pray for
our persecuted brothers. Leave the rest to God.*

FORMULA V 30

2 We héard with our ówn ears, O Gód,
　our fáthers have tóld us the stóry
　of the thíngs you díd in their dáys,
　you yoursélf, in dáys long agó.

3 To plánt them you upróoted the nátions:
　to let them spréad you laid péoples lów.
4 No swórd of their ówn won the lánd;
　no árm of their ówn brought them víctory.
　It was yóur right hánd, your árm
　and the líght of your fáce: for you lóved them.

5 It is yóu, my kíng, my Gód,
　who gránted víctories to Jácob.
6 Through yóu we béat down our fóes;
　in your náme we trámpled our aggréssors.

7 For it was nót in my bów that I trústed
　nor yét was I sáved by my sword:
8 it was yóu who sáved us from our fóes,
　it was yóu who put our fóes to sháme.
9 All day lóng our bóast was in Gód
　and we práised your náme without céasing.

10 Yet nów you have rejécted us, disgráced us:
　you no lónger go fórth with our ármies.
11 You máke us retréat from the fóe
　and our énemies plúnder us at wíll.

12 You máke us like shéep for the sláughter
　and scátter us amóng the nátions.

13 You séll your own péople for nóthing
and máke no prófit by the sále.

14 You máke us the táunt of our néighbours,
the laúghing stock of áll who are néar.
15 Among the nátions, you máke us a býword,
among the péoples a thíng of derísion.

16 All day lóng my disgráce is befóre me:
my fáce is cóvered with sháme
17 at the vóice of the táunter, the scóffer,
at the síght of the fóe and avénger.

*   *   *

18 This beféll us though we hád not forgótten you;
though we hád not been fálse to your cóvenant,
19 though we hád not withdráwn our héarts;
though our féet had not stráyed from your páth.
20 Yet you have crúshed us in a pláce of sórrows
and cóvered us with the shádow of déath.

21 Had we forgótten the náme of our Gód
or strétched out hánds to another gód
22 would not Gód have fóund this óut,
he who knóws the sécrets of the héart?
23 It is for yóu we face déath all day lóng
and are cóunted as shéep for the sláughter.

24 Awáke, O Lord, whý do you sléep?
Aríse, do not rejéct us for éver!
25 Whý do you híde your fáce
and forgét our oppréssion and mísery?

26 For we are bróught down lów to the dúst;
our bódy lies próstrate on the éarth.
27 Stand úp and cóme to our hélp!
Redéem us becáuse of your lóve!

44

Royal wedding song

The Christian feels that he must recite this psalm in praise of the Messiah-King. The Jewish tradition before him did the same, but the Christian has to make a further adjustment: the 'bride' is no longer the old Israel but the new 'Israel of God', the new Jerusalem prepared as a bride adorned for her husband (Apoc. 21: 2). More specifically the liturgy identifies this bride with those who have dedicated their virginity to God. And yet the original meaning of the psalm is beautiful too: love and marriage are seen as noble, God-blessed, things when wife and husband help each other to work 'for the cause of truth and goodness and right'.

FORMULA PS 20
or VI 33 [omit c]

2 My héart overflóws with nóble wórds.
To the kíng I must spéak the sóng I have máde;
my tóngue as nímble as the pén of a scríbe.

3 Yóu are the fáirest of the chíldren of mén
and gráciousness is póured upón your líps:
because Gód has bléssed you for évermóre.

4 O míghty one, gírd your swórd upon your thígh;
in spléndour and státe, 5 ríde on in tríumph
for the cáuse of trúth and góodness and ríght.

Take aím with your bów in your dréad right hánd.
6 Your árrows are shárp: peóples fall benéath you.
The fóes of the kíng fall dówn and lose héart.

7 Your thróne, O Gód, shall endúre for éver.
A scéptre of jústice is the scéptre of your kíngdom.
8 Your lóve is for jústice; your hátred for évil.

Therefore Gód, your Gód, has anóinted yóu
with the óil of gládness abóve other kíngs:
9 your róbes are frágrant with áloes and mýrrh.

From the ívory pálace you are gréeted with músic.
10 The dáughters of kíngs are amóng your lóved ones.
On your ríght stands the quéen in góld of Óphir.

＊　　＊　　＊

11 Lísten, O dáughter, give éar to my wórds:　　[+c]
forgét your own péople and your fáther's hóuse.
12 Só will the kíng desíre your béauty:
Hé is your lórd, pay hómage to hím.

13 And the péople of Týre shall cóme with gífts,
the ríchest of the péople shall séek your fávour.
14 The dáughter of the kíng is clóthed with spléndour,
her róbes embróidered with péarls set in góld.

15 She is léd to the kíng with her máiden compánions.
16 Théy are escórted amid gládness and jóy;
they páss withín the pálace of the kíng.

＊　　＊　　＊

17 Sóns shall be yóurs in pláce of your fáthers:
you will máke them prínces over áll the éarth.

[repeat B]
18 May this sóng make your náme for éver remémbered.
May the péoples práise you from áge to áge.

45

Boundless trust in God's power

*It always gives Israel a feeling of security to remember that her God is
lord of all the armies of heaven and of earth: the same power controls the
universe and subdues hostile nations. That is why the psalmist can speak
in terms of cosmic catastrophe and still be confident. In a tottering world
there is one unshaken Rock, the God of Jacob. And meanwhile a life-
giving stream keeps Jerusalem, the centre of this disturbed world, safe and
prosperous, because where God is, there is peace. One may think of the
baptismal water that washes round the city we call the Church.*

2 Gód is for ús a réfuge and stréngth,
a hélper close at hánd, in tíme of distréss:
3 so wé shall not féar though the éarth should róck,
though the móuntains fáll into the dépths of the séa,
4 even thóugh its wáters ráge and fóam,
even thóugh the móuntains be sháken by its wáves.

The Lórd of hósts is wíth us:
the Gód of Jácob is our strónghold.

5 The wáters of a ríver give jóy to God's cíty,
the hóly pláce where the Móst High dwélls.
6 Gód is withín, it cánnot be sháken;
Gód will hélp it at the dáwning of the dáy.
7 Nátions are in túmult, kíngdoms are sháken;
he lífts his vóice, the éarth shrinks awáy.

8 The Lórd of hósts is wíth us:
·the Gód of Jácob is our strónghold.

9 Cóme, consíder the wórks of the Lórd
the redóubtable déeds he has dóne on the éarth.
10 He puts an énd to wárs over áll the éarth;
the bów he bréaks, the spéar he snáps.
[He búrns the shíelds with fíre.]
11 'Be stíll and knów that Í am Gód,
supréme among the nátions, supréme on the éarth!'

12 The Lórd of hósts is wíth us:
the Gód of Jácob is our strónghold.

46

To God, king of the world

'*Thy kingdom come,*' *we pray, and yet God's kingdom has come already.
But we are thinking of our own acceptance of it, our practical acknowledgment of God's sovereignty. Always however there is comfort in throwing
responsibility on God, as nations once did on their king and military*

leader. *Hence the note of joy in this psalm, and God 'goes up' to the sound of it. No doubt this refers to the procession with the Ark up the Temple hill, but for us there is another 'ascension'. The glorified body of Christ has thrown off the chains of place and time, and he has power to lead us always and everywhere. This is surely a psalm for the feast of the Ascension.*

FORMULA II 28

2 All péoples, cláp your hánds,
   cry to Gód with shóuts of jóy!
3 For the Lórd, the Most Hígh, we must féar,
   great kíng over áll the éarth.

4 He subdúes péoples únder us
   and nátions únder our féet.
5 Our inhéritance, our glóry, is from hím,
   gíven to Jácob out of lóve.

6 God goes úp with shóuts of jóy;
   the Lord goes úp with trúmpet blást.
7 Sing práise for Gód, sing práise,
   sing práise to our kíng, sing práise.

8 God is kíng of áll the éarth,
   Sing práise with áll your skíll.
9 God is kíng óver the nátions;
   God réigns on his hóly thróne.

10 The prínces of the péoples are assémbled
   with the péople of Ábraham's Gód.
   The rúlers of the éarth belong to Gód,
   to Gód who réigns over áll.

47

The invincible city of God

The pagans may speak of their mountain of the gods, terrifying and inaccessible, but the small hill of Zion is dignified by the presence of the one God, and it is a homely place (v. 13). For all its insignificance it can look down on every high place on earth (Psalm 67: 17). There is a strong

*sense of national pride in this psalm but, like the assertions of innocence
in other psalms, it is softened—if not dissolved altogether—by the free
acknowledgment that all comes from God. It is accompanied, too, by a
full acceptance of moral responsibility: the Temple is a place to ponder
God's love for his people, but it is here also that his commands must be
joyfully received.*

FORMULA I 2

2 The Lord is gréat and wórthy to be práised
in the cíty of our Gód.
His holy móuntain *3* ríses in béauty,
the jóy of all the éarth.

Mount Zíon, true póle of the éarth,
the Gréat King's cíty!
4 Gód, in the mídst of its cítadels,
has shówn himself its strónghold.

5 For the kíngs assémbled togéther,
togéther they advánced.
6 They sáw; at ónce they were astóunded;
dismáyed, they fled in féar.

7 A trémbling séized them thére,
like the pángs of bírth,
8 By the éast wind yóu have destróyed
the shíps of Társhish.

9 As we have héard, só we have séen
in the cíty of our Gód,
in the cíty of the Lórd of hósts
which Gód upholds for éver.

10 O Gód, we pónder your lóve
withín your témple.
11 Your práise, O Gód, like your náme
reaches the énds of the éarth.

With jústice your ríght hand is fílled.
12 Mount Zíon rejóices;
the péople of Júdah rejóice
at the síght of your júdgments.

91

13 Walk through Zíon, wálk all róund it;
   count the númber of its tówers.
14 Revíew áll its rámparts,
   exámine its cástles,

   that you may téll the néxt generátion
15 that súch is our Gód,
   our Gód for éver and álways.
   It is hé who léads us.

48

The problem of justice, pain and death

Perhaps the light of subsequent revelation peeps through here. At first we feel that we are back in the over-simplified solution of the problem of evil in Psalm 36: the prosperity of the wicked is no difficulty because it is so shortlived. But there seems to be a sharp distinction in this psalm: wealth cannot buy everlasting life (v. 10), it cannot 'ransom the soul'. But God can ransom it (v. 16). This appears to be more than a confidence in recovery from sickness—of which there is no mention in the psalm. And indeed the solemn opening verses suggest a noteworthy revelation. At least we are on the threshold of the Good News of eternal life.

FORMULA II 53

2 Héar this, áll you péoples,
   give héed, all who dwéll in the wórld,
3 mén both lów and hígh,
   rích and póor alíke!

4 My líps will speak wórds of wísdom.
   My héart is fúll of ínsight.
5 I will túrn my mínd to a párable,
   with the hárp I will sólve my próblem.

＊　　＊　　＊

6 Whý should I féar in evil dáys
   the málice of the fóes who surróund me,

7 mén who trúst in their wéalth,
and bóast of the vástness of their ríches?

8 For nó man can búy his own ránsom,
or pay a príce to Gód for his lífe.
9 The ránsom of his sóul is beyónd him.
10 He cánnot buy lífe without énd,
nor avóid cóming to the gráve.   [repeat D]

11 He knows that wíse men and fóols must both pérish
and léave their wéalth to óthers.
12 Their gráves are their hómes for éver,
their dwélling place from áge to áge,   [repeat D]
though their námes spread wíde through the lánd.

13 In his ríches, mán lacks wísdom: [A+D]
hé is like the béasts that are destróyed.

*   *   *

14 This is the lót of those who trúst in themsélves,
who have óthers at their béck and cáll.
15 Like shéep they are dríven to the gráve,
where déath shall bé their shépherd
and the júst shall becóme their rúlers.   [repeat D]

With the mórning their óutward show vánishes
and the gráve becómes their hóme.
16 But Gód will ránsom me from déath
and táke my sóul to himsélf.

17 Then do not féar when a mán grows rích,
when the glóry of his hóuse incréases.
18 He takes nóthing wíth him when he díes,
his glóry does not fóllow him belów.

19 Though he fláttered himsélf while he líved:
'Men will práise me for áll my succéss,'
20 yet he will gó to jóin his fáthers,
who will néver see the líght any móre.

21 In his ríches, mán lacks wísdom:
hé is like the béasts that are destróyed.

93

49

God's judgment on formalism

Lip-service is not enough, nor is outward ritual observance. The announcement is introduced with solemnity: the poetic device called 'thephany', in which God appears as the lord of nature. With great candour the psalmist presents him as condemning his own people—not for offering sacrifice, though God has no need of it, but for mistaking the outward form for the religion of the heart; honesty, purity, kindliness. These are the true sacrifices of thanksgiving. The lesson is applicable to us all: the liturgy must have self-involvement as its purpose, and the offering we make is the offering of ourselves in union with the sacrifice of Christ. In the morning this is an offering in principle; for the rest of the day it is a confirmation of this offering in practice.

FORMULA II 4

1 The Gód of góds, the Lórd,
   has spóken and súmmoned the éarth,
   from the rísing of the sún to its sétting.
2 Out of Zíon's perfect béauty he shínes.

3 (Our God cómes, he keeps sílence no lónger.)

   Befóre him fíre devóurs,
   aróund him témpest ráges.
4 He cálls on the héavens and the éarth
   to wítness his júdgment of his péople.

5 'Súmmon befóre me my péople
   who made cóvenant with mé by sácrifice.'
6 The héavens procláim his jústice,
   for hé, Gód, is the júdge.

7 'Lísten, my péople, I will spéak;
   Ísrael, I will téstify agáinst you,
   for Í am Gód your Gód.
*21c*I accúse you, láy the charge befóre you.

94

8 I fínd no fáult with your sácrifices,
   your ófferings are álways befóre me.
9 I do not ásk more búllocks from your fárms,
   nor góats from amóng your hérds.

10 For I ówn all the béasts of the fórest,
    béasts in their thóusands on my hílls.
11 I knów all the bírds in the ský,
    all that móves in the fíeld belong to mé.

12 Were I húngry, Í would not téll you,
    for I ówn the wórld and all it hólds.
13 Do you thínk I eat the flésh of búlls,
    or drínk the blóod of góats?

14 Pay your sácrifice of thánksgiving to Gód
    and rénder him your vótive ófferings.
15 Call on mé in the dáy of distréss.
    I will frée you and yóu shall hónour me.'

16 (But Gód sáys to the wícked:)

    'But hów can you recíte my commándments
    and táke my cóvenant on your líps,
17 yóu who despíse my láw
    and thrów my wórds to the wínds,

18 you who sée a thíef and go wíth him;
    who thrów in your lót with adúlterers,
19 who unbrídle your móuth for évil
    and whose tóngue is plótting críme,

20 you who sít and malígn your bróther
    and slánder your ówn mother's són.
21 You do thís, and should Í keep sílence?
    Do you thínk that Í am like yóu?

22 Mark thís, you who néver think of Gód,
    lest I séize you and you cánnot escápe;
23 a sácrifice of thanksgíving hónours me
    and I will shów God's salvátion to the úpright.'

50

Prayer of contrition:
fourth psalm of repentance

The finest of the 'penitential psalms'. Man stands before God guilty but unafraid; indeed, he sees his guilt as a title to mercy and an excuse for hope. A deep sense of sin is already a step towards the sanctity of God —it opens the door for his eager mercy. But Our Lord takes us even further than the psalmist. He teaches us to cry not 'God!' but 'Father!' He bids us think of that father who ran to meet the son who had left him, the father who took the son in his arms and kissed him: 'My son was lost and is found' (Lk. 15: 24). By so much does our trust exceed even that of the psalmist.

3 Have mércy on me, Gód, in your kíndness.
In your compássion blot óut my offénce.
4 O wásh me more and móre from my guílt
and cléanse me fróm my sín.

5 My offénces trúly I knów them;
my sín is álways befóre me.
6 Against yóu, you alóne, have I sínned;
what is évil in your síght I have dóne.

That you may be jústified whén you give séntence
and be withóut repróach when you júdge
7 O sée, in guílt I was bórn,
a sínner was Í concéived.

8 Indéed you love trúth in the héart;
then in the sécret of my héart teach me wísdom
9 O púrify me, thén I shall be cléan;
O wásh me, I shall be whíter than snów.

10 Make me héar rejóicing and gládness,
that the bónes you have crúshed may thríll.

96

11 From my síns turn awáy your fáce
and blót out áll my guílt.

12 A púre heart creáte for me, O Gód,
put a stéadfast spírit withín me.
13 Do not cást me awáy from your présence,
nor depríve me of your hóly spírit.

14 Give me agáin the jóy of your hélp;
with a spírit of férvour sustáin me,
15 that I may téach transgréssors your wáys
and sínners may retúrn to yóu.

16 O réscue me, Gód, my hélper,
and my tóngue shall ríng out your góodness.
17 O Lórd, ópen my líps
and my móuth shall decláre your práise.

18 For in sácrifice you táke no delíght,
burnt óffering from mé you would refúse,
19 my sácrifice, a cóntrite spírit.
A húmbled, contrite héart you will not spúrn.

20 In your góodness, show fávour to Zíon:
rebuíld the wálls of Jerúsalem.
21 Thén you will be pléased with lawful sácrifice,
(burnt ófferings whólly consúmed),
then you will be óffered young búlls on your áltar.

[repeat D]

5 1

The fate of the deceitful

*It is rare to find a psalmist denouncing an individual, and somewhat dis-
concerting; for public worship it is an embarrassment. The only solution
would again seem to be to sing the psalm as it were against oneself. But
perhaps it is not impious to suggest that the first part had better not be
sung at all. When revelation has advanced so much that earlier attitudes*

become unacceptable, it might be preferable to ignore them. It is true that
no word of God can be idle, but this does not mean to say that it speaks
immediately to us. It was enough for the psalmist, necessary perhaps, to
condemn the liar; we have learnt to condemn only the lie.

FORMULA IV 14

3 Whý do you bóast of your wíckedness,   [omit D]
    you chámpion of évil
4 planning rúin áll day lóng,
    (your tóngue like a shárpened rázor),
    you máster of decéit?

5 You love évil móre than góod;   [omit G+D]
    líes more than trúth.
6 You lóve the destrúctive wórd,
    you tóngue of decéit.

7 For thís Gód will destróy you
    and remóve you for éver.
    He will snátch you from your tént and upróot you
    from the lánd of the líving.

8 The júst shall sée and féar.
    They shall láugh and sáy:
9 'So thís is the mán who refúsed
    to take Gód as his strónghold,
    but trústed in the gréatness of his wéalth
    and grew pówerful by his crímes.'

10 But Í am like a grówing olíve trée
    in the hóuse of Gód.
    I trúst in the góodness of Gód
    for éver and éver.

11 I will thánk you for évermóre;
    for thís is your dóing.
    I will procláim that your náme is góod,
    in the présence of your fríends.

52

The fools

FORMULA I 54

2 The fóol has sáid in his héart:
'There is no Gód abóve.'
Their déeds are corrúpt, depráved;
not a góod man is léft.

3 Gód looks dówn from héaven
on the sóns of mén,
to sée if ány are wíse,
if ány seek Gód.

4 Áll have left the ríght páth;
depráved, every óne.
There is nót a góod man léft,
nó, not even óne.

5 Will the évil-doers nót understánd?
They éat up my péople
as thoúgh they were éating bréad;
they néver pray to Gód.

6 Sée how they trémble with féar
without cáuse for féar:
for Gód scatters the bónes of the wícked.
They are shámed, God rejécts them.

7 O that Ísrael's salvátion might cóme from Zíon!
When Gód delívers his péople from bóndage,
then Jácob will be glád and Ísrael rejóice.   [III 49]

See Psalm 13

53

Cry for God's help

The 'name' and the 'power' of God appear as synonymous in the opening verse of our psalm. The 'name' of a person is the expression of his individuality and his peculiar possession. 'May I use your name?' we say when we need access to someone. The 'name' is therefore operative: it unlocks doors. In this way Israel was privileged to use the name of God either to call on him or to threaten its enemies. But now the name that Christians use is even more specific: it is a name greater than all others: Jesus; the name that gives access to God and that threatens everything hostile to our peace.

FORMULA II 8

3 O Gód, sáve me by your náme;
　by your pówer, uphóld my cáuse.
4 O Gód, héar my práyer;
　listén to the wórds of my móuth.

5 For próud men have rísen agáinst me,　　　[omit c]
　rúthless men séek my lífe.
　They háve no regárd for Gód.

6 But Í have Gód for my hélp.
　The Lórd uphólds my lífe.
7 Let the évil recóil upon my fóes:
　yóu who are fáithful, destróy them.

8 I will sácrifice to yóu with willing héart
　and práise your náme for it is góod:
9 for you have réscued me from áll my distréss
　and my éyes have seen the dównfall of my fóes.

54

Distress of a man betrayed by his friend

Distress and discouragement are as strongly marked here as in any psalm in the whole collection. It is true that there is no description of bodily suffering: the wounds of the psalmist go much deeper, and for this reason one feels that the psalm has a more general and a more profound appeal. Moreover, for all the protestations of trust in God we can sense the wavering which attacks us all. We have our Judases, we perhaps are a Judas ourselves. This apostle must have 'walked in the house of God' with Jesus, and yet he betrayed him. Have we? Do we?

FORMULA I 42

2 O Gód, lísten to my práyer,
  do not híde from my pléading,
3 atténd to mé and replý;
  with my cáres, I cannot rést.

I trémble *4* at the shóuts of the fóe,
at the críes of the wícked;
for they bríng down évil upón me.
They assáil me with fúry.

5 My héart is strícken withín me,
  death's térror is ón me,
6 trémbling and féar fall upón me
  and hórror overwhélms me.

7 Ó that I had wíngs like a dóve
  to fly awáy and be at rést.
8 Só I would escápe far awáy
  and take réfuge in the désert.

9 I would hásten to fínd a shélter
  from the ráging wínd,
    from the destrúctive stórm, O Lórd,
10 and from their plótting tóngues.

For Í can see nóthing but víolence
and strífe in the cíty.
11 Níght and dáy they patról
hígh on the city wálls.

It is fúll of wíckedness and évil;
12 it is fúll of sín.
Its stréets are néver frée
from týranny and decéit.

13 If thís had been dóne by an énemy
I could béar his táunts.
If aríval had rísen agáinst me,
I could híde from hím.

14 But it is yóu, my ówn compánion,
my íntimate fríend!
15 (How clóse was the fríendship betwéen us)
We wálked togéther in hármony
in the hóuse of Gód.   [repeat c]

16 May deáth fall súddenly upón them!
Let them gó to the gráve:
for wíckedness dwélls in their hómes
and déep in their héarts.

17 As for mé, I will crý to Gód
and the Lórd will sáve me.
18 Évening, mórning and at nóon
I will crý and lamént.

19 He will delíver my sóul in péace
in the attáck agáinst me:
for thóse who fíght me are mány,
18c but he héars my vóice.

20 Gód will héar and will húmble them,
the etérnal júdge:
for they wíll not aménd their wáys.
They have no féar of Gód.

102

21 The tráitor has túrned against his friends;
he has bróken his wórd.
22 His spéech is sófter than bútter,
but wár is in his héart.   [repeat a+d]
His wórds are smóother than óil,
but they are náked swórds.

23 Entrúst your cáres to the Lórd
and hé will suppórt you.
Hé will néver allów
the júst man to stúmble.

24 But yóu, O Gód, will bring them dówn
to the pít of déath.
Decéitful and blóodthirsty mén
shall not líve half their dáys.

O Lórd, I will trúst in yóu.

55

Unshakable confidence in God

'*You have kept a record of my tears*'. *The sentence is more graphic in the Hebrew: 'You have kept' or 'Keep' my tears in your bottle? This is what professional mourners did: the tears were shed, as it were, by proxy, and left on the grave as evidence of grief. But here the tears are not professional, God knows it, and they are really worth keeping. We can only know what God thinks of human suffering from his Son, God's Word to us: when Jesus saw Martha weeping he started to cry himself (Jn. 11: 33f). But in the end God 'will wipe all tears away' and there will be no more crying (Apoc. 21: 4).*

FORMULA II 4

2 Have mércy on me, Gód, men crúsh me;
they fíght me all day lóng and oppréss me.
3 My fóes crúsh me all day lóng,
for mány fight próudly agáinst me.

103

4 When I féar, I will trúst in yóu,
5 in Gód whose wórd I práise.
　In God I trúst, I sh*ll not féar:
　whát can mortal mán do to mé?

6 All day lóng they distórt my wórds,
　*ll their thóught is to hárm me.
7 They bánd togéther in *mbush,
　track me dówn and séek my lífe.

8 Repáy them, Gód, for their crímes;　　　　　[v 3]
　in your ánger, cast dówn the péoples.
9 You have képt an accóunt of my wánderings;
　you have képt a récord of my téars;
　(áre they not wrítten in your bóok?)　　　[repeat D]
10 Then my fóes will be pút to flíght
　on the dáy that I cáll to yóu.

　This I knów, that Gód is on my síde.　　　[omit D]
11 In Gód, whose wórd I práise,
　[in the Lórd, whose wórd I práise,]
12 in Gód I trúst; I shall not féar:
　whát can mortal mán do to mé?

13 I am bóund by the vóws I have máde you.
　O Gód, I will óffer you práise
14 for you réscued my sóul from déath,
　you képt my féet from stúmbling
　that I may wálk in the présence of Gód
　and enjóy the líght of the líving.

56

In time of danger:
a national lament

The vehemence of the psalmists is a constant surprise:　Heaven knows what some of them must have gone through. Even their joy seems to shine through tears. This individual lament followed by thanksgiving is similar in form and content to the preceding psalm, and indeed to many others.

Nevertheless there is more triumphant joy in the conclusion, accompanied by an almost defiant determination: the 'morning' in the psalms often stands for the dawning of new hope: the psalmist is awake, waiting for it, or rather not waiting but shouting so loud that personified Dawn, that is relief, will have to come.

FORMULA II 4

2 Have mércy on me, Gód, have mércy
for in yóu my sóul has taken réfuge.
In the shádow of your wíngs I take réfuge
till the stórms of destrúction pass bý.

3 I cáll to Gód the Most Hígh,
to Gód who has álways been my hélp.
4 May he sénd from héaven and sáve me
and sháme thóse who assáil me.

May Gód send his trúth and his lóve.

5 My sóul lies dówn among líons,
who would devóur the sóns of mén.
Their téeth are spéars and árrows,
their tóngue a shárpened swórd.

6 O Gód, aríse above the héavens;
may your glóry shine on eárth!

7 They láid a snáre for my stéps,   [1 6]
my sóul was bowed dówn.
They dúg a pít in my páth
but féll in it themsélves.

8 My héart is réady, O Gód,   [IV 5]
my héart is réady.
I will síng, I will síng your práise.
9 Awáke my sóul,
awáke lýre and hárp,
I will awáke the dáwn.

10 I will thánk you Lórd among the péoples,
among the nátions I will práise you

105

11 for your lóve réaches to the héavens
and your trúth to the skíes.

12 O Gód, aríse above the héavens;
may your glóry shine on eárth!

57

Condemnation of injustice

Faced with injustice on a national scale the psalmist does not measure his language. God, the supreme judge of his people, is being betrayed by his delegates, made like Adam in God's own likeness and, like Adam, distorting it. What could the pagans think of a theocracy like this? Only the destruction of these caricatures of divine justice can clear the image of God which Israel should present to the world. Through them 'the name of God is blasphemed'. There is great responsibility for all who belong to God's community: their light must shine before men.

FORMULAS III 12
and VI 11

2 Do you trúly speak jústice, you who hóld divine pówer?
Do you méte out fair júdgment to the sóns of mén?
3 Nó, in your héarts you devíse injústice;
your hánds déal out víolence to the lánd.

4 In their wíckedness théy have gone astráy from their
bírth: [VI 11]
they wándered among líes as sóon as they were bórn.
5 Their vénom is líke the vénom of the snáke;
they are héedless as the ádder that túrns a deaf éar
6 lést it should cátch the snáke-charmer's vóice,
the vóice of the skílful déaler in spélls.

7 O Gód, bréak the téeth in their móuths,
téar out the fángs of these wíld beasts, O Lórd!
8 Let them vánish like wáter that rúns awáy:
let them wíther like gráss that is tródden underfóot:
9 let them bé like the snáil that dissólves into slíme:
like a wóman's miscárriage that néver sees the sún.

10 Befóre they pút forth thórns, like a brámble,
let them be swépt awáy, gréen wood or drý!
11 The júst shall rejóice at the síght of véngeance;
they shall báthe their féet in the blóod of the wícked.
12 'Trúly,' men shall sáy, 'the júst are rewárded.
Trúly there is a Gód who does jústice on éarth.'

58

Appeal to God, the stronghold

*It is possible that in this psalm, as in Psalm 57, the thought is on a
national plane: that the 'foes' are as much a danger to the whole nation
as they are to the psalmist himself: 'Kill them lest my people be seduced.'
But, unlike the previous psalm, the enemies seem to come from outside
(The 'traitors' of v. 6 are paralleled with 'the nations'). We too have
our enemies from outside: there are so many hostile influences in our age
as in every other, pariah dogs, persistent and ready to snap. We cannot
live behind closed doors but we have inside us our own immunity—or rather
the immunity that comes from God to those who are aware of him.*

FORMULA II 8

2 Réscue me, Gód, from my fóes;
protéct me from thóse who attáck me.
3 O réscue me from thóse who do évil
and sáve me from blóod-thirsty mén.

4 See, they líe in wáit for my lífe;
powerful mén band togéther agáinst me.
For no offénce, no sín of mine, Lórd,
5 for no guílt of mine they rúsh to take their stánd.

Awáke, come to my áid and sée!
6 Lord of hósts, you are Ísrael's Gód.
Rouse yoursélf and púnish the nátions;
show no mércy to évil tráitors.

7 Each évening they come báck like dógs.
They hówl and róam about the cíty,
they prówl in séarch of fóod,
they snárl till they háve their fíll.

8 Sée how they gábble open-móuthed;
  their líps are fílled with ínsults.
  'For whó,' they sáy, 'will héar us?'   [repeat B]
9 But yóu, Lord, will láugh them to scórn.
  You make líght of áll the nátions.

10 O my Stréngth, it is yóu to whom I túrn,   [omit C]
   for yóu, O Gód, are my strónghold,
11 the Gód who shóws me lóve.

   O Gód, cóme to my áid
   and let me lóok in tríumph on my fóes.
12 God, kíll them lest my péople be sedúced;
   róut them by your pówer, lay them lów.

   It is yóu, O Lórd, who are our shíeld.
13 For the síns of their móuths and their líps,
   for the cúrses and líes that they spéak
   lét them be cáught in their príde.

14 Destróy them, Lórd, in your ánger.
   Destróy them till théy are no móre.
   Let men knów that Gód is the rúler
   over Jácob and the énds of the éarth.

15 Each évening they come báck like dógs.
   They hówl and róam about the cíty,
16 they prówl in séarch of fóod,
   they snárl till they háve their fíll.

17 As for mé, I will síng of your stréngth
   and each mórning accláim your lóve
   for yóu have béen my strónghold,
   a réfuge in the dáy of my distréss.

18 O my Stréngth, it is yóu to whom I túrn,   [omit C]
   for yóu, O Gód, are my strónghold,
   the Gód who shóws me lóve.

59

After a defeat

This time it is certainly the nation that laments: the occasion might even be identified with the fall of Jerusalem in 586 B.C. It may be that the difficult verses 8-11 which have an archaic ring have been taken over from some earlier composition: in this section we read the divine oracle given in answer to the initial appeal. David's kingdom and sphere of influence is God's possession: he can do what he likes with Moab, and Edom belongs to him (he has 'thrown his sandal' over it, cf. Ruth 4: 7). He will guard these jealously. God's property is always safe as long as it remains true to itself.

FORMULA II 48

3 O Gód, you have rejécted us and bróken us.
Yóu have been ángry; come báck to us.

4 You have máde the earth quáke, torn it ópen.
Repáir what is sháttered for it swáys.
5 You have inflícted hárdships on your péople
and máde us drink a wíne that dázed us.

6 You have gíven those who féar you a sígnal
to flée from the énemy's bów.
7 O cóme and delíver your fríends,
hélp with your ríght hand and replý.

*　　*　　*

8 From his hóly place Gód has made this prómise;
[omit B]
'I will tríumph and divíde the land of Shéchem,
I will méasure out the válley of Súccoth.

9 Gílead is míne and Manásseh,
Éphraim I táke for my hélmet,
Júdah for my commánder's stáff.
109

10 Móab I will úse for my wáshbowl;
on Édom I will plánt my shóe.
Over the Phílistines I will shóut in tríumph.'

11 But who will léad me to cónquer the fórtress?
Who will bríng me face to fáce with Édom?
12 Will you útterly rejéct us, O Gód,
and no lónger márch with our ármies?

13 Give us hélp agáinst the fóe:
for the hélp of mán is váin.
14 With Gód wé shall do brávely
and hé will trámple down our fóes.

See Psalm 107

60

Prayer of an exile

*We are back now among emphatically personal psalms (60-3) though in
this one it seems that the song is intended for the use of the king. For Israel,
when it did not forget, the king was only holding the kingdom on behalf
of God: two guards flanked his throne and their names were 'God's
Love' and 'God's Protection'. It must however be admitted that vv. 2-6
sound like the reflections—almost mystical—of a devout Israelite and that
these have been offered to the king for his own meditation. None who have
any authority at all—and most have some—can afford to ignore the Rock
on which they stand.*

FORMULAS I 54 and II 53

2 O Gód, héar my crý!
Lísten to my práyer!
3 From the énd of the éarth I cáll:
my héart is fáint.

On the róck too hígh for me to réach
sét me on hígh,
4 O yóu who have béen my réfuge,
my tówer against the fóe.

5 Let me dwéll in your tént for éver
and híde in the shélter of your wíngs.
6 For yóu, O Gód, hear my práyer,
grant me the héritage of thóse who féar you.

7 May you léngthen the lífe of the kíng:
may his yéars cover mány generátions.
8 May he éver sit enthróned before Gód:
bid lóve and trúth be his protéction.

9 So I will álways práise your náme
and dáy after dáy fulfil my vóws.

61

God, the rock of strength:
a psalm of confidence

The one solid foundation is God; the wise man does not build on sand, or the winds and floods will bring his house down (Mt. 7: 24ff). There is no alternative (the words 'alone' and 'only' are repeated so often: cf. vv. 2, 3, 6, 7, 12). This 'rock' is opposed to human help which is illusory, weightless: dictatorship, success in war, a prosperous business, all these are inadequate even when they last—which is not for long. There is an atmosphere of tranquil assurance in this psalm which we miss in many others where we meet with almost frenzied appeal. In the psalter we can usually find a prayer to suit our moods.

FORMULAS I 59 and IV 58
2 In God alóne is my sóul at rést;
my hélp comes from hím.
3 He alóne is my róck, my strónghold,
my fórtress: I stand fírm.

4 How lóng will you áll attack one mán
to bréak him dówn,
as thóugh he were a tóttering wáll,
or a túmbling fénce?

III

5 Their plán is ónly to destróy:
they take pléasure in líes.
With their móuth they útter bléssing
but in their héart they cúrse.

6 In God alóne be at rést, my sóul;
for my hópe comes from hím.
7 He alóne is my róck, my strónghold,
my fórtress: I stand fírm.

8 In Gód is my sáfety and glóry,   [IV 58]
the róck of my stréngth.
Take réfuge in Gód 9 all you péople.
Trúst him at áll times.
Póur out your héarts befóre him
for Gód is our réfuge.

10 Cómmon folk are ónly a bréath,
gréat men an illúsion.
Pláced in the scáles, they ríse;
they weigh léss than a bréath.

11 Dó not put your trúst in oppréssion
nor vain hópes on plúnder.
Dó not set your héart on ríches
even whén they incréase.

12 For Gód has sáid only óne thing: [IV 58]
only twó do I knów:
that to Gód alóne belongs pówer
13 and to yóu, Lord, lóve;
and that yóu repáy each mán
accórding to his déeds.

62

Longing for God

*As in Psalm 60 we have unexpected reference to the king at the end of a
psalm that is even more mystical—perhaps the warmest and most intimate
of the expressions of love for God in the entire psalter. The image of a
'dry and weary land', which possibly suggested the superscription: 'When*

David was in the wilderness of Judah', is surely no more, and no less, than a description of the dreariness of life without God. In vv. 4-9 the images accumulate: to love God is to live fully, to feast, to rest content, to be under a protecting wing, to embrace, to be embraced. Even St. John of the Cross could scarcely do better than this.

2 O Gód, you are my Gód, for you I lóng;
   for yóu my sóul is thírsting.
   My bódy pínes for yóu
   like a drý, weary lánd without wáter.
3 So I gáze on yóu in the sánctuary
   to sée your stréngth and your glóry.

4 For your lóve is bétter than lífe,
   my líps will spéak your práise.
5 So I will bléss you áll my lífe,
   in your náme I will líft up my hánds.
6 My sóul shall be fílled as with a bánquet,
   my móuth shall práise you with jóy.

7 On my béd I remémber yóu.
   On yóu I múse through the níght
8 for yóu have béen my hélp;
   in the shádow of your wíngs I rejóice.
9 My sóul clíngs to yóu;
   your ríght hand hólds me fást.

10 Those who séek to destróy my lífe
   shall go dówn to the dépths of the éarth.
11 They shall be pút into the pówer of the swórd
   and léft as the préy of the jáckals.
12 But the kíng shall rejóice in Gód;
   (all that swéar by hím shall be bléssed)
   for the móuth of líars shall be sílenced.

63

The defeat of God's enemies

It dismays us sometimes that the psalmist should descend from the warmth of his love for God to a cold denunciation of his own enemies (this disappointment is felt most strongly in Psalm 138: 19ff). We wonder how we can make the whole psalm our own. There is a real problem here which is insoluble unless we realise how God had to deal with a people who saw the world in black and white, and who did not easily distinguish the sin from the sinner. For the people of today with a little more insight into the influences suffered by the human mind, unqualified condemnation is not possible. Do not judge others or you will be judged yourselves. Consequently, the denunciation must be transposed into another key, even turned against ourselves, or rather against everything in ourselves that robs us of that thirst for God which the psalmist feels so acutely.

FORMULAS II 10 and V 9

2 Hear my vóice, O Gód, as I compláin,
    guard my lífe from dréad of the fóe.
3 Híde me from the bánd of the wícked,
    from the thróng of thóse who do évil.

4 They shárpen their tóngues like swórds;
    they áim bitter wórds like árrows
5 to shóot at the ínnocent from ámbush,
    shóoting súddenly and récklessly.

6 They schéme their évil cóurse;
    they conspíre to lay sécret snáres.
    They sáy: 'Whó will sée us?
7 Whó can séarch out our crímes?'

*   *   *

He will séarch who séarches the mínd   [v 9]
    and knóws the dépths of the héart.
8 Gód has shót them with his árrow
    and déalt them súdden wóunds.
9 Their ówn tongue has bróught them to rúin
    and áll who sée them móck.

10 Thén will áll men féar;
   they will téll what Gód has dóne.
   They will únderstánd God's déeds.
11 The júst will rejóice in the Lórd
   and flý to hím for réfuge.
   All the úpright héarts will glóry.

64

Song of springtime:
a psalm of worship

*Learning from the Exodus, Israel knew God as saviour. When she changed
her way of life from that of a semi-nomadic people to that of settled agri-
culture, the recurrence of sowing and harvest, of early rain and summer
ripening, enabled her to see him as the giver of life and creator. The vision
was unclouded and immediate; no technicality of modern farming was
there to blunt the edge of wonder. For Israel it was God alone who dressed
the flowers. Perhaps we should try to recapture this sense of God working
through the winter to bring new life and new colour: this same power
raised Christ's body and it will raise our own, working throughout the
winter of our lives.*

FORMULA I 29

2 To yóu our práise is dúe
  in Zíon, O Gód.
  To yóu we páy our vóws,
3 you who héar our práyer.

  To yóu all flésh will cóme
4 with its búrden of sín.
  Too héavy for ús, our offénces,
  but you wípe them awáy.

5 Blessed is hé whom you chóose and cáll
  to dwéll in your cóurts.
  We are fílled with the bléssings of your hóuse,
  of your hóly témple.

6 You kéep your plédge with wónders,
  O Gód our sáviour,
  the hópe of áll the éarth
  and of fár distant ísles.

7 You uphóld the móuntains with your stréngth,
  you are gírded with pówer.
8 You stíll the róaring of the séas,
  (the róaring of their wáves)   [repeat D]
  and the túmult of the péoples.

9 The énds of the éarth stand in áwe
  at the síght of your wónders.
  The lánds of súnrise and súnset
  you fíll with your jóy.

10 You cáre for the éarth, give it wáter,
  you fíll it with ríches.
  Your ríver in héaven brims óver
  to províde its gráin.

  And thús you províde for the éarth;
11 You drénch its fúrrows,
  you lével it, sóften it with shówers,
  you bléss its grówth.

12 You crówn the yéar with your góodness.   [omit B]
  Abúndance flóws in your stéps,
13 in the pástures of the wílderness it flóws.

  The hílls are gírded with jóy,
14 the méadows cóvered with flócks,
  the válleys are décked with whéat.
  They shoút for jóy, yes, they síng.

65

A people's thanksgiving

The 'we' of vv. 2-12 changes abruptly to 'I' in v. 13. If this is not a combination of two independent psalms one must assume that a leader (the king?) is speaking for his people or that some private individual has used a national psalm to introduce his own prayer. On the whole it seems

*better to suppose two psalms later joined by an editor. The difficulty is
not so much the change of provision (the strong sense of community might
account for that) as the complete change of tone from national to personal:
in the first half the nation has been led through the Red Sea and across the
Jordan and through subsequent trials (unspecified: v. 12 leaves a feeling
of abruptness); in the second an individual has come through some personal
distress with the help of God. Common to both parts is relief and joy.*

FORMULA II 24

1 Cry out with jóy to Gód all the éarth,
2 O síng to the glóry of his náme.
O rénder him glórious práise.
3 Say to Gód: 'How treméndous your déeds!

Becáuse of the gréatness of your stréngth
your énemies crínge befóre you.
4 Befóre you all the éarth shall bów;
shall síng to you, síng to your náme!'

5 Come and sée the wórks of Gód,
treméndous his déeds among mén.
6 He túrned the séa into dry lánd,
they pássed through the ríver dry-shód.

Let our jóy then bé in hím;
7 he rúles for éver by his míght.
His éyes keep wátch over the nátions:
let rébels not ríse agáinst him.

8 O péoples, bléss our Gód,
let the vóice of his práise resóund,
9 of the Gód who gave lífe to our sóuls
and képt our féet from stúmbling.

10 For yóu, O Gód, have tésted us,
you have tríed us as sílver is tríed:
11 you léd us, Gód, into the snáre;
you láid a heavy búrden on our bácks.

12 You lét men ríde over our héads;   [omit B]
we wént through fíre and through wáter
but thén you bróught us relíef.

13 Burnt óffering I bríng to your hóuse;
to yóu I will páy my vóws,
14 the vóws which my líps have úttered,
which my móuth spóke in my distréss.

15 I will óffer burnt ófferings of fátlings
with the smóke of búrning ráms.
I will óffer búllocks and góats.

16 Come and héar, áll who fear Gód.
I will téll what he díd for my sóul:
17 to hím I críed alóud,
with high práise réady on my tóngue.

18 If there had béen évil in my héart,
the Lórd would nót have lístened.
19 But trúly Gód has lístened;
he has héeded the vóice of my práyer.

20 Blessed be Gód who did nót reject my práyer
nor withhóld his lóve from mé.

66

Harvest song

The occasion of this happy song is a successful harvest, but the psalmist can rise above selfish considerations. There is an astonishing universality here that reminds us of the third section of Isaiah. It is a very 'ecumenical' psalm indeed. The thin coating we call the soil covers the whole earth; it binds all nations together in a common interest; from this they all get their living. But the triumph of a good harvest—or industrial prosperity— should make one think of places where the harvest fails: God is the same God there, and man no less his image. If God rules the whole world with justice, man must try to imitate him. Ecumenism and economics are sometimes the same thing.

FORMULA II 24

2 O Gód, be grácious and bléss us
and let your fáce shed its líght upón us.
3 So will your wáys be knówn upon éarth
and all nátions learn your sáving hélp.

4 Let the péoples práise you, O Gód;
let áll the péoples práise you.

5 Let the nátions be glád and exúlt
for you rúle the wórld with jústice.
With fáirness you rúle the péoples,
you guíde the nátions on éarth.

6 Let the péoples práise you, O Gód;
let áll the péoples práise you.

7 The éarth has yíelded its frúit
for Gód, our Gód, has bléssed us.
8 May Gód still gíve us his bléssing
till the énds of the éarth revére him.

Let the péoples práise you, O Gód;
let áll the péoples práise you.

67

The journey of God's people: triumphant hymn of thanks

The most picturesque—and obscure—of all the psalms. In the Roman liturgy, it particularly celebrates the Ascension of Christ. And no wonder: it is a hymn fit for the climax-victory of God fighting for his people and there is a wild joy running through it. God rides on the clouds but marches across the desert too; he feeds his starving people; he takes willing captives with him to his holy place on the hill; his might is in the skies. In the same way the Son of Man whose chariot was a cloud (Dan. 7: 13, cf. Mt. 26: 64) went on foot through the wilderness and fed his people there (Jn. 6); when he ascended he took a host of 'captives' with him (Eph. 4: 8), and his power is felt from heaven where he sits at the Father's right hand.

FORMULA VI 33 (omit E)

2 Let Gód aríse, let his fóes be scáttered.
Let thóse who háte him flée befóre him.

3 As smóke is blown awáy so will théy be blown awáy;
like wáx that mélts befóre the fíre,
so the wícked shall pérish at the présence of Gód.

4 But the júst shall rejóice at the présence of Gód,
they shall exúlt and dánce for jóy.
5 O síng to the Lórd, make músic to his náme;
make a híghway for hím who rídes on the clóuds.
Rejóice in the Lórd, exúlt at his présence.

6 Fáther of the órphan, defénder of the wídow,
súch is Gód in his hóly pláce.
7 Gód gives the lónely a hóme to líve in;
he léads the prísoners fórth into fréedom:
but rébels must dwéll in a párched lánd.

8 When you wént forth, O Gód, at the héad of your
péople,
when you márched across the désert, *9* the éarth
trémbled:
the héavens mélted at the présence of Gód,
at the présence of Gód, Ísrael's Gód.

10 You póured down, O Gód, a génerous ráin:
when your péople were stárved you gáve them new
lífe.
11 It was thére that your péople fóund a hóme,
prepáred in your góodness, O Gód, for the póor.

12 The Lórd gives the wórd to the béarers of good tídings:
'The Almíghty has deféated a númberless ármy
13 and kíngs and ármies are in flíght, in flíght
while yóu were at rést amóng the shéepfolds.'

14 At hóme the wómen alréady share the spóil.
They are cóvered with sílver as the wíngs of a dóve,
its féathers brílliant with shíning góld
15 and jéwels fláshing like snów on Mount Zálmon.

16 The móuntains of Báshan are míghty móuntains;
hígh-ridged móuntains are the móuntains of Báshan.
17 Why lóok with énvy, you hígh-ridged móuntains,
at the móuntain where Gód has chósen to dwéll?
It is thére that the Lórd shall dwéll for éver.

18 The cháriots of Gód are thóusands upon thóusands.
The Lórd has come from Sínai to the hóly pláce.
19 You have góne up on hígh; you have táken cáptives,
recéiving mén in tríbute, O Gód,
even thóse who rebél, into your dwélling, O Lórd.

20 May the Lórd be bléssed dáy after dáy.
He béars our búrdens, Gód our sáviour.
21 This Gód of oúrs is a Gód who sáves.
The Lórd our Gód holds the kéys of déath.
22 And Gód will smíte the héad of his fóes,
the crówn of thóse who persíst in their síns.

23 The Lord sáid: 'I will bríng them báck from Báshan;
I will bríng them báck from the dépth of the séa.
24 Thén your féet will tréad in their blóod
and the tóngues of your dógs take their sháre of the fóe.'

25 They sée your sólemn procéssion, O Gód,
the procéssion of my Gód, of my kíng, to the sánctuary:
26 the síngers in the fórefront, the musícians coming lást,
betwéen them, máidens sóunding their tímbrels.

27 'In féstive gátherings, bléss the Lórd;
bless Gód, O yóu who are Ísrael's sóns.'
28 There is Bénjamin, léast of the tríbes, at the héad,
Júdah's prínces, a míghty thróng,
Zébulun's prínces, Náphtali's prínces.

29 Show fórth, O Gód, show fórth your míght,
your míght, O Gód, which you have shówn for ús
30 for the sáke of your témple hígh in Jerúsalem
may kíngs cóme to you brínging their tríbute.

31 Thréaten the wíld beast that dwélls in the réeds,
the bánds of the míghty and lórds of the péoples.
Lét them bow dówn óffering sílver.
Scátter the péoples who delíght in wár.   [+E]
32 Prínces will máke their wáy from Égypt:
Ethiópia will strétch out her hánds to Gód.

33 Kíngdoms of the éarth, sing to Gód, praise the Lórd
34 who rídes on the héavens, the áncient héavens.
He thúnders his vóice, his míghty vóice.
35 Cóme, acknówledge the pówer of Gód.

His glóry is on Ísrael; his míght is in the skíes.
36 Gód is to be féared in his hóly pláce.
Hé is the Lórd, Ísrael's Gód.
Hé gives stréngth and pówer to his péople.

Bléssed be Gód!

68

Cry from the depths of sorrow

An abrupt descent from the joy of the previous psalm to the depths of misery: whoever put these two psalms side by side had a strong sense of contrast. Perhaps he thought that ecstatic joy can go on too long and must have its corrective. For a Hebrew this must be surprising enough, for the Christian it is very pointed indeed. In Psalm 67 he sees the triumph of Christ; in Psalm 68 he sees the struggle that came, that had to come, before it: It was necessary that the Christ should suffer, and in this way enter his glory. We cannot put all these words on the lips of Jesus: there was no 'sinful folly' (v. 6) in him, and he would never have uttered the curses of vv. 23-9—instead he cried 'Father, forgive them'. But the evangelist John invites us to think of Jesus as we recite this psalm (Jn. 2: 17; cf. also Mt. 27: 34) and we would be wise to take his hint.

FORMULA I 6

2 Sáve me, O Gód,
for the wáters have rísen to my néck.

3 I have súnk into the múd of the déep
and there is nó fóothold.
I have éntered the wáters of the déep
and the wáves overwhélm me.

4 I am wéaried with áll my crýing,
my thróat is párched.
My éyes are wásted awáy
from lóoking for my Gód.

5 More númerous than the háirs on my héad
are those who háte me without cáuse.
Thóse who attáck me with líes
are too múch for my stréngth.

Hów can Í restóre
what I have néver stólen?
6 O Gód, you know my sínful fólly;
my síns you can sée.

7 Let those who hópe in you nót be put to sháme
through mé, Lord of hósts:
let not thóse who séek you be dismáyed
through mé, God of Ísrael.

8 It is for yóu that I súffer táunts,   [v 3]
that sháme cóvers my fáce,
9 that I have becóme a stránger to my bróthers,
an álien to my ówn mother's sóns.
10 I búrn with zéal for your hóuse
and táunts against yóu fall on mé.

11 When I afflíct my sóul with fásting
they máke it a táunt agáinst me.
12 When I pút on sáckcloth in móurning
thén they máke me a býword,
13 the góssip of mén at the gátes,
the súbject of drúnkards' sóngs.

14 Thís is my práyer to yóu,   [iv 5]
my práyer for your fávour.
In your great lóve, ánswer me, O Gód,
with your hélp that never fáils:
15 réscue me from sínking in the múd;
sáve me from my fóes.

Sáve me from the wáters of the déep
16 lest the wáves overwhélm me.
Dó not let the déep engúlf me
nor déath clóse its móuth on me.

17 Lord, ánswer, for your lóve is kínd; [v 3]
in your compássion, túrn towárds me.
18 Do not híde your fáce from your sérvant;
answer quíckly for I am in distréss.
19 Come clóse to my sóul and redéem me;
ránsom me préssed by my fóes.

20 You knów how they táunt and deríde me;
my oppréssors are áll befóre you.
21 Táunts have bróken my héart;
I have réached the énd of my stréngth.
I lóoked in váin for compássion,
for consólers; not óne could I fínd.

22 For fóod they gáve me póison;
in my thírst they gave me vínegar to drínk.
23 Let their táble be a snáre to thém
and their féstive bánquets a tráp.
24 Let their éyes grow dím and blínd;
let their límbs trémble and sháke.

25 Póur out your ánger upón them,
let the héat of your fúry overtáke them.
26 Let their cámp be léft désolate;
let nó one dwéll in their ténts:
27 for they pérsecute óne whom you strúck;
they incréase the páin of him you wóunded.

28 Chárge them with guílt upon guílt;
let them néver be found júst in your síght.
29 Blot them óut from the bóok of the líving;
do not enról them amóng the júst.
30 As for mé in my póverty and páin
let your hélp, O Gód, lift me úp.

31 I will práise God's náme with a sóng; [II 4]
I will glórify hím with thanksgíving.
32 A gíft pleasing Gód more than óxen,
more than béasts prepáred for sácrifice.

33 The póor when they sée it will be glád [v 3]
and Gód-seeking héarts will revíve;

34 for the Lórd lístens to the néedy
and does not spúrn his sérvants in their cháins.
35 Let the héavens and the éarth give him práise,
the séa and all its líving créatures.

36 For Gód will bring hélp to Zíon
and rebuíld the cíties of Júdah
and mén shall dwéll there in posséssion.
37 The sóns of his sérvants shall inhérit it;
thóse who love his náme shall dwéll there.

69

Prayer of trust and appeal

It will be noticed that this psalm is a repetition of Psalm 39: 14-18 almost word for word, but here the 'Lord' of Psalm 39 becomes 'God' in vv. 2-5. As a result the devout are invited to cry 'God ("Elohim") is great', and this loses the force of 'The Lord ("Yahweh") is great'. Yahweh is the 'proper name' of God which distinguishes him from the gods (elohim) of the nations which he has conquered easily whether they were the gods of Egypt or the gods of Babylon. The Exodus and the Return from Babylon have proved this. Christians use the same name still: Jesus (Yehoshua) means 'Yahweh is Saviour'; he is the Lord we are bidden to acknowledge (1 Jn. 4: 15).

FORMULA I 2

2 O Gód, make háste to my réscue,
Lord, cóme to my áid!
3 Lét there be sháme and confúsion
on thóse who seek my lífe.

O lét them turn báck in confúsion,
who delíght in my hárm,
4 let them retréat, cóvered with sháme,
who jéer at my lót.

5 Lét there be rejóicing and gládness
for áll who séek you.
Let them sáy for ever: 'Gód is gréat,'
who lóve your saving hélp.

6 As for mé, wrétched and póor,
cóme to me, O Gód.
Yóu are my réscuer, my hélp,
O Lórd, do not deláy.

70

Prayer in old age

An old man looks back on his life; he was taught at his mother's knee to put his trust in God always, and he has not forgotten (vv. 6, 17); but has God forgotten him? His enemies say 'yes'; he knows better. And yet he is anxious: even a short life has its crisis and he has lived a long time, and God seems very far away. Though the psalmist expresses himself in the conventional language so familiar to us from other psalms this does not conceal his very real distress, and we can imagine here the situation of Job himself. One learns with age how powerfully the resilience of youth contributed even to religious optimism; God slowly and gently teaches us to do without it, and this unconscious young confidence in ourselves having done its work is now removed. If old age wishes it, God is closer than ever: the trust is purified.

FORMULA II 10

1 In yóu, O Lórd, I take réfuge;
let me néver be pút to sháme.
2 In your jústice réscue me, frée me:
pay héed to mé and sáve me.

3 Be a róck where Í can take réfuge,   [v 9, omit D]
a míghty strónghold to sáve me;
for yóu are my róck, my strónghold.
4 Frée me from the hánd of the wícked,
from the gríp of the unjúst, of the oppréssor.

5 It is yóu, O Lórd, who are my hópe,
my trúst, O Lórd, since my yóuth.
6 On yóu I have léaned from my bírth,
from my móther's womb yóu have been my hélp.
My hópe has álways been in yóu.

126

7 My fáte has filled mány with áwe
but yóu are my stróng réfuge.
8 My líps are filled with your práise,
with your glóry áll the day lóng.   [repeat D]
9 Do not rejéct me nów that I am óld;
when my stréngth fails dó not forsáke me.

10 For my énemies are spéaking abóut me;
those who wátch me take cóunsel togéther
11 saying: 'Gód has forsáken him; fóllow him,
séize him; there is nó one to sáve him.'
12 O Gód, do not stáy far óff:
my Gód, make háste to hélp me!

13 Let thém be put to sháme and destróyed,   [1 14]
all thóse who seek my lífe.
Let them be cóvered with sháme and confúsion,
all thóse who seek to hárm me.

14 But as for mé, I will álways hópe   [v 9, omit D]
and práise you móre and móre.
15 My líps will téll of your jústice
and dáy by dáy of your hélp
(though Í can néver tell it áll).

16 I will decláre the Lórd's mighty déeds
procláiming your jústice, yours alóne.
17 O Gód, you have táught me from my yóuth
and I procláim your wónders stíll.

18 Nów that I am óld and grey-héaded,   [v 9]
dó not forsáke me, Gód.
Let me téll of your pówer to all áges,
praise your stréngth 19 and jústice to the skíes,
tell of yóu who have wórked such wónders.
O Gód, whó is líke you?

20 You have búrdened me with bítter tróubles
but you will gíve me báck my lífe.
You will ráise me from the dépths of the éarth;
21 you will exált me and consóle me agáin.

22 So I will gíve you thánks on the lýre　　　　[v 9]
for your fáithful lóve, my Gód.
To yóu will I síng with the hárp
to yóu, the Hóly One of Ísrael.
23 When I síng to you my líps shall rejóice
and my sóul, which yóu have redéemed.

24 And áll the day lóng my tóngue
shall téll the tále of your jústice:
for théy are put to sháme and disgráced,
all thóse who séek to hárm me.

71

The kingdom of peace

*A picture of the future ideal king, or an idealistic picture of the reigning
king? In any case it outlines the king-Messiah as Israel would hope him
to be: after all, every new Davidic King must have seemed a potential
Messiah. The courtly compliments—if this is what they are—are quite
deliberately extravagant: the whole of the inhabited earth, the soil itself,
pays him homage. But not unwillingly. The king buckles on no sword as
he does in Psalm 44: there is not a weapon mentioned, except the weapons
of integrity (v. 7) and sympathy (vv. 12-14). Surely this psalm prepares
God's people for a king who would tell his followers to put the sword back
in the scabbard?*

FORMULA I 37

1 O Gód, give your júdgment to the kíng,
to a kíng's son your jústice,
2 that he may júdge your péople in jústice
and your póor in right júdgment.

3 May the móuntains bring forth péace for the péople
and the hílls, jústice.
4 May he defénd the póor of the péople
and save the chíldren of the néedy　　　　[repeat D]
(and crúsh the oppréssor).

5 He shall endúre like the sún and the móon
  from áge to áge.
6 He shall descénd like ráin on the méadow,
  like ráindrops on the éarth.

7 In his dáys jústice shall flóurish
  and péace till the móon fails.
8 He shall rúle from séa to séa,
  from the Great Ríver to earth's bóunds.

9 Befóre him his énemies shall fáll,
  his fóes lick the dúst.
10 The kíngs of Társhish and the séa coasts
  shall páy him tríbute.

The kíngs of Shéba and Séba
shall bríng him gífts.
11 Before hím all kíngs shall fall próstrate,
  all nátions shall sérve him.

12 For he shall sáve the póor when they crý
  and the néedy who are hélpless.
13 Hé will have píty on the wéak
  and save the líves of the póor.

14 From oppréssion he will réscue their líves,
  to hím their blood is déar.
15 (Lóng may he líve,   [repeat B]
  may the góld of Shéba be gíven him.)
  They shall práy for hím without céasing   [repeat C]
  and bléss him all the dáy.

16 May córn be abúndant in the lánd
  to the péaks of the móuntains.
  May its frúit rústle like Lébanon;
  may men flóurish in the cíties
  like gráss on the éarth.   [repeat D]

17 May his náme be bléssed for éver
  and endúre like the sún.
  Every tríbe shall be bléssed in hím,
  all nátions bless his náme.

*   *   *

18 Bléssed be the Lórd, God of Ísrael,
who alóne works wónders,
19 ever bléssed his glórious náme.
Let his glóry fill the éarth.

Amén! Amén!   [repeat D]

72

The problem of innocent suffering

We are not used to bitter words in the psalms, but we have them here. All the more remarkable is the reaction at the end, than which there is no higher mystical attitude in the psalter. Indeed, we may have here a confidence in a future life with God beyond the grave. If so, revelation has taken a great leap and the problem of suffering is solved—or nearly solved. One thing is certain: the psalmist has supreme confidence in God, yet he seems quite prepared to see the wicked prosper and himself suffer as long as this life lasts. If the conclusion is not explicitly drawn, it is there implicitly. This psalm will always be relevant: the human situation described here is familiar to us all; so is the temptation, so is the necessary faith.

FORMULA V 9

1 How góod God ís to Ísrael,
to thóse who are púre of héart.
2 Yet my féet came clóse to stúmbling,
my stéps had álmost slípped
3 for Í was filled with énvy of the próud
when I sáw how the wícked prósper.

4 For thém there áre no páins;   [II 10]
their bódies are sóund and sléek.
5 They háve no sháre in men's sórrows;
they áre not strícken like óthers.

6 So they wéar their príde like a nécklace,
they clóthe themsélves with víolence.
7 Their héarts overflów with málice,
their mínds séethe with plóts.

130

8 They scóff; they spéak with málice;
from on hígh they plán oppréssion.
9 They have sét their móuths in the héavens
and their tóngues dictáte to the éarth.

10 So the péople túrn to fóllow them   [v 9]
and drínk in áll their wórds.
11 They sáy: 'Hów can God knów?
Dóes the Most Hígh take any nótice?'
12 Lóok at them, súch are the wícked,
but untróubled, they grów in wéalth.

*   *   *

13 How úseless to kéep my heart púre
and wásh my hánds in ínnocence,
14 when I was strícken áll day lóng,
suffered púnishment dáy after dáy.

15 Then I sáid: 'If I should spéak like thát,
I should betráy the ráce of your sóns.'

16 I stróve to fáthom this próblem,
too hárd for my mínd to understánd,
17 until I píerced the mýsteries of Gód
and understóod what becómes of the wícked.

*   *   *

18 How slíppery the páths on which you sét them;
You m´ke them slíde to destrúction.
19 How súddenly they cóme to their rúin,
wiped oút, destróyed by térrors.
20 Like a dréam one wákes from, O Lórd,
when you wáke you dismíss them as phántoms.

21 And só when my héart grew embíttered
and whén I was cút to the quíck,
22 I was stúpid and díd not understánd,
no bétter than a béast in your síght.

131

23 Yet I was álways ín your présence;
   you were hólding me bý my right hánd.
24 You will guíde me bý your cóunsel
   and só you will léad me to glóry.

25 What élse have I in héaven but yóu?
   Apart from yóu I want nóthing on éarth.
26 My bódy and my héart faint for jóy;
   Gód is my posséssion for éver.

27 All thóse who abándon you shall pérish;
   you will destróy all thóse who are fáithless.
28 To bé near Gód is my háppiness.
   I have máde the Lord Gód my réfuge.
   I will téll of áll your wórks
   at the gátes of the cíty of Zíon.

73

God's people mourn over the ruined temple: a national lament

The problem of evil again, but this time from the nation's point of view —and there is no hint that the nation has deserved its punishment. What is at stake, therefore, is the reputation of God himself: at least this is how the psalmist cunningly puts it. The occasion of this lament could be the first truly religious persecution in history—under Antiochus Epiphanes in 168 B.C.—but on the whole the arguments favour the destruction of Jerusa. .n by the Babylonians in 586. But naturally it is the ruin of the temple that the psalmist describes: it should move God to action if his own house has been attacked. The psalm is unhappily all too apposite at the present day: we pray for the Church of Silence.

FORMULA VI 33
1 Whý, O Gód, have you cást us off for éver?
   Whý blaze with ánger at the shéep of your pásture?
2 Remémber your péople whom you chóse long agó,
   the tríbe you redéemed to be your ówn posséssion,
   the móuntain of Zion where you máde your dwélling.

3 Turn your stéps to these pláces that are útterly rúined!
　The énemy has laid wáste the whóle of the sánctuary.
4 Your fóes have made úproar in your hóuse of práyer:
　they have sét up their émblems, their fóreign émblems,
5 hígh abóve the éntrance to the sánctuary.

　Their áxes *6* have báttered the wóod of its dóors.
　They have strúck togéther with hátchet and píckaxe.
7 O Gód, they have sét your sánctuary on fíre:
　they have rázed and profáned the pláce where you
　　dwéll.
8 They sáid in their héarts: 'Let us útterly crúsh them:
　let us búrn every shríne of Gód in the lánd.'
9 There is no sígn from Gód, nor háve we a próphet,
　we have nó one to téll us how lóng it will lást.

10 How lóng, O Gód, is the énemy to scóff?
　is the fóe to insúlt your náme for éver?
11 Whý, O Lórd, do you hóld back your hánd?
　Whý do you kéep your ríght hand hídden?

12 Yet Gód is our kíng from tíme pást,
　the gíver of hélp through áll the lánd.
13 It was yóu who divíded the séa by your míght,
　who sháttered the héads of the mónsters in the séa.

14 It was yóu who crúshed Levíathan's héads
　and gáve him as fóod to the úntamed béasts.
15 It was yóu who ópened spríngs and tórrents;
　it was yóu who dríed up éver-flowing rívers.

16 Yóurs is the dáy and yóurs is the níght.
　It was yóu who appóinted the líght and the sún:
17 it was yóu who fíxed the bóunds of the éarth:
　yóu who máde both súmmer and wínter.

18 Remémber this, Lórd, and see the énemy scóffing;
　a sénseless péople insúlts your náme.
19 Do not gíve Ísrael, your dóve, to the háwk
　nor forgét the life of your póor ones for éver.

20 Remémber your cóvenant; every cáve in the lánd
   is a pláce where víolence mákes its hóme.
21 Do not lét the oppréssed retúrn disappóinted;
   let the póor and the néedy bléss your náme.

22 Aríse, O Gód, and defénd your cáuse!
   Remémber how the sénseless revíle you all the dáy.
23 Dó not forgét the clámour of your fóes,
   the dáily incréasing úproar of your fóes.

74

Judge of the world

*The basic attitude of man towards God is evidently humility: it appears
here as the one criterion of judgment. But it is a mistake to think that any
passage of Scripture exhausts its topic, and the tableau of judgment in
Matthew 25 makes active charity the test. Yet even here the element of
humility comes in, because the charity is exercised for the 'least' of Christ's
brothers. In short it seems that all can escape judgment who ask for
mercy: perhaps this is why the Pharisees are attacked in the gospels and
not the harlots. This judgment is always threatening, or rather it is
operating continually in individual lives; but here it is spoken of as a
crisis for humanity at large and one thinks of the choice for or against
that Christ proposed and proposes to the world; the proud 'prince of this
world is already judged' (Jn. 16: 11) and the meek shall possess the land.*

FORMULA II 18
2 We give thánks to yóu, O Gód,   [omit B]
  we give thánks and cáll upon your náme.
  We recóunt your wónderful déeds.

*   *   *

3 'When I réach the appóinted tíme,
  thén I will júdge with jústice.
4 Though the éarth and all who dwéll in it may róck,
  it is Í who uphóld its píllars.

5 To the bóastful I say: "Do not bóast,"
  to the wícked: "Do not fláunt your stréngth,

134

6 do not fláunt your stréngth on hígh.
Do not spéak with ínsolent príde." '

7 For néither from the éast nor from the wést,
nor from désert or móuntains comes júdgment,
8 but Gód himsélf is the júdge.
One he húmbles, anóther he exálts.

9 The Lórd holds a cúp in his hánd,
full of wíne, fóaming and spíced.
He póurs it; they drínk it to the drégs:
all the wícked on the éarth must dráin it.

10 As for mé, I will rejóice for éver
and sing psálms to Jácob's Gód.
11 He shall bréak the pówer of the wícked,
while the stréngth of the júst shall be exálted.

75

Song after victory

The immense power of God is wielded with infinite delicacy: it comes down at speed to crush everything that opposes its strength but leaves those who know their own weakness quite untouched. For these the divine omnipotence is not a terrifying thing because it fights on their side; their weakness is God's opportunity to show his strength: 'My power appears to perfection where there is weakness' (2 Cor. 12: 9). God never displays his power to impress but always to rescue, just as the incarnate Word used his power for the sick and the hungry only because he was sorry for them, and walked on the lake only to rejoin and calm his frightened disciples. If the psalmist delights in God the Warrior we can hardly blame him: it is only a child boasting of his Father's strength.

FORMULA V 17

2 Gód is made knówn in Júdah;
in Ísrael his náme is gréat.
3 He sét up his tént in Jerúsalem
and his dwélling pláce in Zíon.
4 It was thére he bróke the flashing árrows,
the shíeld, the swórd, the ármour.

5 Yóu, O Lórd, are respléndent,
  more majéstic than the éverlasting móuntains.
6 The wárriors, despóiled, slept in déath;
  the hánds of the sóldiers were pówerless.
7 At your thréat, O Gód of Jácob,
  hórse and ríder lay stúnned.

8 Yóu, you alóne, strike térror.
  Who shall stánd when your ánger is róused?
9 You úttered your séntence from the héavens;
  the éarth in térror was stíll
10 when Gód aróse to júdge,
  to sáve the húmble of the éarth.

11 Men's ánger will sérve to práise you;
  its survívors surróund you in jóy.
12 Make vóws to your Gód and fulfíl them.
  Let all pay tríbute to hím who strikes térror,
13 who cúts short the bréath of prínces,
  who strikes térror in the kíngs of the éarth.

76

God's dealings with Israel:
prayer of a perplexed man

One feels that the psalmist is distressed not on his own behalf but by the plight of his people. When he recalls the great days when the nation was brought to birth through God's mercy and his power he wonders what can have happened to this child who seemed so promising. He ends on a pathetic, nostalgic note. It does not seem that the nation has been unfaithful, otherwise he would not be as puzzled as he clearly is: again it is the problem of evil on a national scale; the right hand of God once outstretched now seems to have been withdrawn. There is no answer offered: the Lord has given, the Lord has taken away, that is all. This is so often the case with nations and with individuals. Blessed be the name of the Lord for what he gave, even though he has taken it away.

FORMULA V 39

2 I crý alóud to Gód,
  cry alóud to Gód that he may héar me.

3 In the dáy of my distréss I sought the Lórd.   [omit ᴇ]
My hánds were raised at níght without céasing;
my sóul refúsed to be consóled.
4 I remémbered my Gód and I gróaned.
I póndered and my spírit fáinted.

5 You withhéld sléep from my éyes.
I was tróubled, I cóuld not spéak.
6 I thóught of the dáys of long agó
and remémbered the yéars long pást.
7 At níght I músed within my héart.
I póndered and my spírit quéstioned.

8 'Will the Lórd rejéct us for éver?
Will he shów us his fávour no móre?
9 Has his lóve vánished for éver?
Has his prómise cóme to an énd?
10 Does Gód forgét his mércy
or in ánger withhóld his compássion?'

11 I said: 'Thís is what cáuses my gríef;
that the wáy of the Most Hígh has chánged.'
12 I remémber the déeds of the Lórd,
I remémber your wónders of óld,
13 I múse on áll your wórks
and pónder your míghty déeds.

14 Your wáys, O Gód, are hóly.
What gód is gréat as our Gód?
15 Yóu are the Gód who works wónders.
Yóu showed your pówer among the péoples.
16 Your stróng arm redéemed your péople,
the sóns of Jácob and Jóseph.

17 The wáters sáw you, O Gód,
the wáters sáw you and trémbled;
the dépths were móved with térror.
18 The clóuds póured down ráin,
the skíes sent fórth their vóice;
your árrows fláshed to and fró.

137

19 Your thúnder rólled round the ský,
your fláshes líghted up the wórld.
The éarth was móved and trémbled
20 when your wáy léd through the séa,
your páth through the míghty wáters
and nó one sáw your fóotprints.

21 You guíded your péople like a flóck
by the hánd of Móses and Áaron.

77

God's patience and man's ingratitude: the lesson of past history

The four-beat rhythm of Israel's history: divine generosity, human ingratitude, correction, renewed generosity, is an enlarged picture of individual experience. God rarely shows his hand in such a way that men are forced to recognise it in the events of history: this needs a thoughtful and grateful heart. And even then we easily forget. In the past God's people had found themselves threatened first by the sea, then by the desert. Flood and drought, too much and too little, luxury and penury, have always been the enemies of the people of God: 'Give me neither poverty nor riches: give me only the food I need' is the sober prayer of the Book of Proverbs. But when God rescues from the two extremes there are still the dangers of mediocrity. We can soon forget the urgent prayers in past crisis and the way God heard them: but every day must be seen as a crisis in which God intervenes: 'Give us this day our daily bread!'

FORMULA II 53

1 Give héed, my péople to my téaching;
turn your éar to the wórds of my móuth.
2 I will ópen my móuth in a párable
and revéal hidden léssons of the pást.

3 The thíngs we have héard and understóod,
the thíngs our fáthers have tóld us
4 thése we will not híde from their chíldren
but will téll them to the néxt generátion:

138

the glóries of the Lórd and his míght
and the márvellous déeds he has dóne,
5 the wítness he gáve to Jácob,
the láw he estáblished in Ísrael.

He gáve a commánd to our fáthers
to máke it knówn to their chíldren
6 that the néxt generátion might knów it,
the chíldren yét to be bórn.

7 They tóo should aríse and tell their sóns
that they tóo should set their hópe in Gód
and néver forgét God's déeds
but kéep every óne of his commánds:

8 so that théy might not be líke their fáthers,
a defíant and rebéllious ráce,
a ráce whose héart was fíckle,
whose spírit was unfáithful to Gód.

*　　*　　*

9 The sons of Éphraim, ármed with the bów,
turned báck in the dáy of báttle.
10 They fáiled to kéep God's cóvenant
and would not wálk accórding to his láw.

11 They forgót the thíngs he had dóne,
the márvellous déeds he had shówn them.
12 He did wónders in the síght of their fáthers,
in Égypt, in the pláins of Zóan.

13 He divíded the séa and led them thróugh
and made the wáters stand úp like a wáll.
14 By dáy he léd them with a clóud:
by níght, with a líght of fíre.

15 He splít the rócks in the désert.
He gave them pléntiful drínk as from the déep.
16 He made stréams flow óut from the róck
and made wáters run dówn like rívers.

*　　*　　*

17 Yet still they sínned agáinst him;
   they defíed the Most Hígh in the désert.
18 In their héart they put Gód to the tést
   by demánding the fóod they cráved.

19 They éven spóke against Gód.   [omit c]
   They sáid: 'Is it póssible for Gód
   to prepáre a táble in the désert?

20 It was hé who strúck the róck,
   water flówed and swépt down in tórrents.
   But cán he álso give us bréad?
   Can he províde méat for his péople?'

21 When he héard this the Lórd was ángry.
   A fíre was kíndled against Jácob,
   his ánger róse against Ísrael
22 for háving no fáith in Gód;   [repeat D]
   for refúsing to trúst in his hélp.

23 Yet he commánded the clóuds abóve
   and ópened the gátes of héaven.
24 He ráined down mánna for their fóod,
   and gáve them bréad from héaven.

25 Mere mén ate the bréad of ángels.
   He sént them abúndance of fóod:
26 he made the éast wind blów from héaven
   and róused the sóuth wind by his míght.

27 He ráined fóod on them like dúst,
   winged fówl like the sánds of the séa.
28 He let it fáll in the mídst of their cámp
   and áll aróund their ténts.

29 So they áte and hád their fíll;
   for he gáve them áll they cráved.
30 But befóre they had sáted their cráving,
   while the fóod was stíll in their móuths,

31 God's ánger róse agáinst them.   [omit c]
   He sléw the stróngest amóng them,
   struck dówn the flówer of Ísrael.

140

32 Despíte this they wént on sínning;
   they hád no fáith in his wónders:
33 so he énded their dáys like a bréath
   and their yéars in súdden rúin.

34 When he sléw them thén they would séek him,
   retúrn and séek him in éarnest.
35 They would remémber that Gód was their róck,
   Gód the Most Hígh their redéemer.

36 But the wórds they spóke were mere fláttery;
   they líed to hím with their líps.
37 For their héarts were not trúly wíth him;
   they wére not fáithful to his cóvenant.

38 Yet hé who is fúll of compássion
   forgáve their sín and spáred them.
   So óften he héld back his ánger
   when he míght have stírred up his ráge.

39 He remémbered they were ónly mén,
   a breath that pásses néver to retúrn.

*   *   *

40 How óften they defíed him in the wílderness
   and cáused him páin in the désert!

41 Yet agáin they put Gód to the tést
   and gríeved the Hóly One of Ísrael.
42 They díd not remémber his déeds
   nor the dáy he sáved them from the fóe;

43 when he wórked his míracles in Égypt,
   his wónders in the pláins of Zóan:
44 when he túrned their rívers into blóod,
   made their stréams impóssible to drínk.

45 He sent dóg-flies agáinst them to devóur them
   and swárms of frógs to molést them.
46 he gáve their cróps to the grúb,
   the frúit of their lábour to the lócust.

47 He destróyed their vínes with háil,
their sýcamore trées with fróst.
48 He gáve up their cáttle to plágue,
their flócks and hérds to péstilence.

49 He túrned on them the héat of his ánger,
fúry, ráge and hávoc,
a tróop of destróying ángels.
50 He gáve free cóurse to his ánger.

He díd not spáre them from déath
but gáve their líves to the plágue.
51 He strúck all the fírst-born in Égypt,
the finest flówer in the dwéllings of Hám.

52 Then he bróught forth his péople like shéep;
he guíded his flóck in the désert.
53 He led them sáfely with nóthing to féar,
while the séa engúlfed their fóes.

54 So he bróught them to his hóly lánd,
to the móuntain which his ríght hand had wón.
55 He dróve out the nátions befóre them,
and divíded the lánd for their héritage.

Their ténts he gáve as a dwélling
to éach one of Ísrael's tríbes.

*   *   *

56 Still they put Gód to the próof and defíed him;
they refúsed to obéy the Most Hígh.

57 They stráyed, as fáithless as their fáthers,
like a bów on which the árcher cannot cóunt.
58 With their móuntain shrínes they ángered him;
made him jéalous with the ídols they sérved.

59 God sáw and was fílled with fúry:
he útterly rejécted Ísrael.
60 He forsóok his dwélling place in Shíloh,
the tént where he líved among mén.

61 He gáve his árk into captívity,
   his glorious árk into the hánds of the fóe.
62 He gáve up his péople to the swórd,
   in his ánger agáinst his chósen ones.

63 So wár devóured their young mén,
   their máidens had no wédding sóngs;
64 their príests féll by the swórd
   and their wídows máde no lamént.

65 Then the Lórd awóke as if from sléep,
   like a wárrior overcóme with wíne.
66 He strúck his fóes from behínd
   and pút them to éverlasting sháme.

67 He rejécted the tént of Jóseph;
   He did not chóose the tríbe of Éphraim
68 but he chóse the tribe of Júdah,
   the híll of Zíon which he lóves.

69 He búilt his shríne like the héavens,
   or like the éarth which he made fírm for éver.
70 And he chóse Dávid his sérvant
   and tóok him awáy from the shéepfolds.

71 From the cáre of the éwes he cálled him
   to be shépherd of Jácob his péople,
   of Ísrael his ówn posséssion.
72 He ténded them with blámeless héart,
   with discérning mínd he léd them.   [repeat D]

78

National lament over the destruction of Jerusalem

*Like Psalm 74 this one almost certainly refers to the fall of Jerusalem
in 586 B.C. Unlike Psalm 74 there is a confession of guilt—the guilt of
an earlier generation. It is interesting that this ingredient should enter the
solution of the problem of suffering: Has this man sinned—or his parents?
And indeed we may blame our ancestors for some of our condition, so long
as we realise that we may, and do, contribute to the unhappiness of our*

143

children. We are the context into which they will be born for better or worse. But the psalmist evidently does not wish to call God's attention to the sins of his own generation except in passing (v. 9); and there is a further devout ingenuity about him when (v. 10) he reminds God of what people will say if he deserts his people. As if God cared! But such a prayer is very human and no doubt raises a smile in heaven.

FORMULA VI II

1 O Gód, the nátions have inváded your lánd,
   they háve profáned your hóly témple.
   They have máde Jerúsalem a héap of rúins.
2 They have hánded óver the bódies of your sérvants
   as fóod to féed the bírds of héaven
   and the flésh of your fáithful to the béasts of the éarth.

3 They have póured our blóod like wáter in Jerúsalem,
   nó one is léft to búry the déad.
4 Wé have becóme the táunt of our néighbours,
   the móckery and scórn of thóse who surróund us.
5 How lóng, O Lórd? Will you be ángry for éver,
   how lóng will your ánger búrn like fíre?

6 Póur out your ráge on the nátions,   [v 9]
   the nátions that dó not knów you.
   Póur out your ráge on the kíngdoms
   that dó not cáll on your náme;
7 for théy have devóured Jácob
   and laid wáste the lánd where he dwélls.

8 Do not hóld the guílt of our fáthers agáinst us. [vi 17]
   Lét your compássion hásten to méet us
   wé are léft in the dépths of distréss.
9 O Gód our sáviour, cóme to our hélp,
   cóme for the sáke of the glóry of your náme.
   O Lórd our Gód, forgíve us our síns;   [repeat F]
   réscue ús for the sáke of your náme.

10 Whý should the nátions say: 'Whére is their Gód?'
                          [omit D]
   Let us sée the nátions aróund us repáid
   with véngeance for the blóod of your sérvants that was
     shéd!

144

11 Let the gróans of the prísoners cóme befóre you;
let your stróng arm repríeve those condémned to díe.

12 Pay báck to our néighbours séven times óver   [omit D]
the táunts with whích they táunted you, O Lórd.
13 But wé, your péople, the flóck of your pásture,
will gíve you thánks for éver and éver.
We will téll your práise from áge to áge.

79

Plea for the return of God's favour

The theme is much the same as in the preceding psalm, but the scene shifts
to the northern kingdom where the axe fell first: Samaria was overrun in
721 B.C. and colonised with a mixed population of idolatrous immigrants:
so many weeds in the garden of God. What has he done to his vineyard?
Understandably enough—and other psalms have taught us to expect it—
there is no mention of the wild grapes this chosen vine had produced (Is.
5: 1-7), and the psalmist dares to ask 'why?' The prophet Amos could
provide the answer: thirty years before this time he had scourged the luxury
and oppression of the ruling classes (Am. 6: 4-7). But we have to sympathise with our psalmist: he at least has learnt the lesson that to brood
over sins committed is a worthless exercise.

FORMULA V 9

2 O shépherd of Ísrael, héar us,
you who léad Jóseph's flóck,
shine fórth from your chérubim thróne
3 upon Éphraim, Bénjamin, Manásseh.
O Lórd, róuse up your míght,
O Lórd, cóme to our hélp.

4 Gód of hósts, bríng us báck;
let your fáce shine on ús and wé shall be sáved.

5 Lórd God of hósts, how lóng
will you frówn on your péople's pléa?
6 You have féd them with téars for their bréad,
an abúndance of téars for their drínk.

7 You have máde us the táunt of our néighbours,
our énemies láugh us to scórn.

8 Gód of hósts, bríng us báck;
let your fáce shine on ús and wé shall be sáved.

9 You bróught a víne out of Égypt; [omit a+D]
to plánt it you dróve out the nátions.
10 Befóre it you cléared the gróund;
it took róot and spréad through the lánd.

11 The móuntains were cóvered with its shádow,
the cédars of Gód with its bóughs.
12 It strétched out its bránches to the séa,
to the Great Ríver it strétched out its shóots.

13 Then whý have you bróken down its wálls?
It is plúcked by áll who pass bý.
14 It is rávaged by the bóar of the fórest,
devóured by the béasts of the fíeld.

15 God of hósts, turn agáin, we implóre,
look dówn from héaven and sée.
Vísit this víne 16 and protéct it,
the víne your ríght hand has plánted.
17 Men have búrnt it with fíre and destróyed it.
May they pérish at the frówn of your fáce.

18 May your hánd be on the mán you have chósen,
the mán you have gíven your stréngth.
19 And we shall néver forsáke you agáin:
give us lífe that we may cáll upon your náme.

20 Gód of hósts, bríng us báck;
let your fáce shine on ús and wé shall be sáved.

80

Festal song in harvest time

The complaints of the divine voice (vv. 12-13) sound strangely out of place in a psalm which opens so joyfully. There is a second incongruity: the trumpet or ram's horn (jobel, hence our 'jubilee') is to be sounded 'at the new moon, when the moon is full'. To deal with the second puzzle first: it is possible that the harvest-feast of Tabernacles is referred to here (celebrated at the full moon in the lunar month of September-October) and also the first day of the New Year (the first day of the same month). The first difficulty is lessened if we suppose that the people sing vv. 2-6 exultantly, but a prophet in the sanctuary reminds them that joy should be tempered with self-mistrust: if past experience teaches anything it should teach them this—and ourselves as well.

FORMULA II 31

2 Ring out your jóy to Gód our stréngth,
  shout in tríumph to the Gód of Jácob.

3 Raise a sóng and sóund the tímbrel,
  the swéet-sounding hárp and the lúte,
4 blów the trúmpet at the néw moon,
  when the móon is fúll, on our féast.

5 For thís is Ísrael's láw,
  a commánd of the Gód of Jácob.
6 He impósed it as a rúle on Jóseph,
  when he went óut against the lánd of Égypt.

A vóice I did not knów said to mé:
7 'I fréed your shóulder from the búrden;
  your hánds were fréed from the lóad.
8 You cálled in distréss and I sáved you.

I ánswered, concéaled in the stórm cloud,
  at the wáters of Meríbah I tésted you.
9 Lísten, my péople, to my wárning,
  O Ísrael, if ónly you would héed!

147

10 Let there bé no fóreign god amóng you,
no wórship of an álien gód.
11 Í am the Lórd your Gód,
who bróught you from the lánd of Égypt.
Ópen wide your móuth and I will fíll it.   [repeat D]

12 But my péople did not héed my vóice
and Ísrael wóuld not óbey,
13 so I léft them in their stúbbornness of héart
to fóllow their ówn desígns.

14 Ó that my péople would héed me,
that Ísrael would wálk in my wáys!
15 At ónce I would subdúe their fóes,
turn my hánd agáinst their énemies.

16 The Lord's énemies would crínge at their féet
and their subjéction would lást for éver.
But Ísrael I would féed with finest whéat
and fíll them with hóney from the róck.'

81

Judgment on corrupt authority

God presides over every court, however eminent the judges. It is possible that the judges mentioned here are the 'beggarly elemental spirits', dictatorial 'beings that by nature are no gods' (Col. 4: 8ff) but in effect are worshipped by so many: the stars, for example, have their devotees still, and horoscopes are not unpopular. This interpretation may seem to be supported by vv. 5-7. On the other hand, vv. 2-4 suggest more commonplace magistrates and, though the evangelists are capable of adjusting old sayings to the new situation, one feels that the original sense remains in Jn. 10: 34. From this text Jesus gently vindicated his own claim to be Son of God with authority delegated by his Father. He would not blind his interlocutors with revelation: time was needed before the full meaning of this pregnant title could be declared.

FORMULA V 17

1 God stánds in the divíne assémbly.
In the mídst of the góds he gives júdgment.

2 'How lóng will you júdge unjústly
and fávour the cáuse of the wícked?

3 Do jústice for the wéak and the órphan,
defénd the afflícted and the néedy.

4 Réscue the wéak and the póor;
set them frée from the hánd of the wícked.

5 Unpercéiving, they grópe in the dárkness
and the órder of the wórld is sháken.

6 I have sáid to you: "Yóu are góds
and áll of you, sóns of the Most Hígh."

7 And yét, you shall díe like mén,
you shall fáll like ány of the prínces.'

8 Aríse, O Gód, judge the éarth,
for yóu rule áll the nátions.

82

A nation's appeal to God
for help against destruction

This reads like a very old psalm indeed, and one is tempted to date it as early as the eighth, or even the tenth century before Christ. There is an international conspiracy against Israel; but this is not the first time: the ancient enemies mentioned in the books of Exodus and Judges (e.g. Jg. 4 and 7) thought they could destroy a people that belonged to God. But the Lord of creation has cosmic weapons at his disposal: 'the stars in their courses fought against Sisera' (Jg. 5: 14) as 'the sun has stood still' for Joshua (Jos. 10: 12). The powers of evil are impotent against the people of God so long as these remember to use the right kind of sword, which is the sword of the spirit.

FORMULA V 17

2 O Gód, dó not keep sílent,
do not be dúmb and unmóved, O Gód,

3 for your énemies ráise a túmult.
Those who háte you líft up their héads.

4 They plót agáinst your péople,
conspíre against thóse you lóve.
5 They say: 'Cóme, let us destróy them as a nátion;
let the náme of Ísrael be forgótten.'
6 They conspíre with a síngle mínd,
they make cómmon allíance agáinst you,

7 the cámps of Édom and of Íshmael,
the cámps of Móab and Hágar,
8 the lánd of Ámmon and Ámalek,
Philístia, with the péople of Týre.
9 Assýria tóo is their álly
and joins hánds with the sóns of Lót.

10 Tréat them like Mídian, like Sísera,
like Jábin at the Ríver Kíshon,
11 the mén who were destróyed at Éndor,
whose bódies rótted on the gróund.

12 Make their cáptains like Óreb and Zééb,
all their prínces like Zébah and Zalmúnna,
13 the mén who sáid: 'Let us táke
the fíelds of Gód for ourselvés.'
14 My Gód, scátter them like cháff,
dríve them like stráw in the wínd!

15 As fíre that búrns away the fórest,
as the fláme that sets the móuntains abláze,
16 dríve them awáy with your témpest
and fíll them with térror at your stórm.
17 Cóver their fáces with sháme,
till they séek your náme, O Lórd.

18 Shame and térror be théirs for éver,
lét them be disgráced, let them pérish!
19 Let them knów that your náme is the Lórd,
the Most Hígh over áll the éarth.

83

Love and longing for God's temple

The home of God on earth! What can this mean? There can be no change in God: he cannot move into a new house. No, the change is in human things. God is everywhere already but consecrates certain places where men can meet him and feel his presence more intimately. There is a power there without which not a sparrow falls to the ground, but also a peace that encourages the sparrow to build its nest. Such a home of God stood on the hill of Zion—a weary climb for the pilgrim at the end of his journey but strengthening him when he paused to raise his eyes. But the end of every pilgrimage lies further off, and it is a very weary climb for some, weary for all. Our city is heaven, but in a sense it is here too: 'You have come to mount Zion, to the city of the living God' (Heb. 12: 22), because the Word was made flesh and dwelt amongst us: in a new sense the earth is the Lord's.

FORMULA II 8

2 How lóvely is your dwélling pláce,
   Lórd, Gód of hósts.

3 My sóul is lónging and yéarning,
   is yéarning for the cóurts of the Lórd.
   My héart and my sóul ring out their jóy
   to Gód, the líving Gód.

4 The spárrow hersélf finds a hóme
   and the swállow a nést for her bróod;
   she láys her yóung by your áltars,
   Lord of hósts, my kíng and my Gód.

5 They are háppy, who dwéll in your hóuse,
   for éver sínging your práise.
6 They are háppy, whose stréngth is in yóu,
   in whose héarts are the róads to Zíon.

7 As they gó through the Bítter Válley
   they máke it a pláce of spríngs
   [the áutumn rain cóvers it with bléssings].

151

8 They wálk with éver growing stréngth,
they will sée the God of góds in Zíon.

9 O Lórd God of hósts, hear my práyer,
give éar, O Gód of Jácob.
10 Turn your éyes, O Gód, our shíeld,
lóok on the fáce of your anóinted.

11 Óne day withín your cóurts
is bétter than a thóusand elsewhére.
The thréshold of the hóuse of Gód
I prefér to the dwéllings of the wícked.

12 For the Lord Gód is a rámpart, a shíeld;
he will gíve us his fávour and glóry.
The Lórd will not refúse any góod
to thóse who wálk without bláme.

13 Lórd, Gód of hósts,
háppy the mán who trusts in yóu!

84

The coming age of peace and justice

'*Are we to continue in sin so that grace can abound? By no means!*'
(*Rom. 6: 1*). *This would be folly no doubt; and yet we may pray with
the psalmist: You have forgiven us before, now forgive us again. It seems
that in his goodness God has established a dangerous precedent! So much
the better: a confident love pervades this psalm and we are consoled. The
harsh word 'justice' is the only discord, but it is a notoriously hard word
to translate: it is no more opposed to 'peace' than 'mercy' is opposed to
'faithfulness' (v. 11); indeed it is very close to it even before the two
'embrace'. 'Justice' is in effect the loving purpose of God for all mankind—
in this sense Jesus 'fulfils all justice' (Mt. 3: 15); by this 'justice'
everything falls happily into place. Now 'peace' is 'the tranquillity that
comes from order', and peace comes to men who are the objects of God's
goodwill (Lk. 2: 14), that is to say of his 'justice'. In the Christian
dispensation these two have embraced indeed.*

2 O Lórd, you once fávoured your lánd
and revíved the fórtunes of Jácob,
3 you forgáve the guílt of your péople
and cóvered áll their síns.
4 You avérted áll your ráge,
you cálmed the héat of your ánger.

5 Revíve us now, Gód, our hélper!
Put an énd to your gríevance agáinst us.
6 Will you be ángry with ús for éver,
will your ánger néver céase?

7 Will you nót restóre again our lífe
that your péople may rejóice in yóu?
8 Let us sée, O Lórd, your mércy
and gíve us your sáving hélp.

*   *   *

9 I will héar what the Lord Gód has to sáy,
a vóice that spéaks of péace,
péace for his péople and his fríends
and those who túrn to hím in their héarts.
10 His help is néar for thóse who féar him
and his glóry will dwéll in our lánd.

11 Mércy and faíthfulness have mét;
jústice and péace have embráced.
12 Fáithfulness shall spríng from the éarth
and jústice look dówn from héaven.

13 The Lórd will máke us prósper
and our éarth shall yíeld its frúit.
14 Jústice shall márch befóre him
and péace shall fóllow his stéps.

85

Loyalty in God's service

This is a gentle psalm, a little muted in tone without cries for help or loud shouts of anguish. There are enemies about—there always are—but God is not asked to destroy them (a refreshing change!); he is asked only to 'turn and take pity' on the persecuted. The first seven verses are the perfect prayer; God could scarcely resist it: the psalmist never stops asking, and he is rightly sure that such a God could never stop giving. He persuades God with his mother's virtues too (v. 16). It is a very homely psalm.

FORMULA II I

1 Turn your éar, O Lórd, and give ánswer
  for Í am póor and néedy.
2 Preserve my lífe, for Í am fáithful:
  save the sérvant who trústs in yóu.

3 You are my Gód, have mércy on me, Lórd,
  for I crý to you áll the day lóng.
4 Give jóy to your sérvant, O Lórd,
  for to yóu I líft up my sóul.

5 O Lórd, you are góod and forgíving,
  full of lóve to áll who cáll.
6 Give héed, O Lórd, to my práyer
  and atténd to the sóund of my vóice.

7 In the dáy of distréss I will cáll
  and súrely yóu will replý.
8 Among the góds there is nóne like you, O Lórd;
  nor wórk to compáre with yóurs.

9 All the nátions shall cóme to adóre you
  and glórify your náme, O Lórd:
10 for you are gréat and do márvellous déeds,
  yóu who alóne are Gód.

154

11 Shów me, Lórd, your wáy   [omit c]
so that Í may wálk in your trúth.
Guide my héart to féar your náme.

12 I will práise you, Lord my Gód, with all my héart
and glórify your náme for éver;
13 for your lóve to mé has been gréat:
you have sáved me from the dépths of the gráve.

14 The próud have rísen agáinst me;   [omit c]
rúthless men séek my lífe:
to yóu they páy no héed.

15 But yóu, God of mércy and compássion,
slów to ánger, O Lórd,
abóunding in lóve and trúth,
16 túrn and take píty on mé.

O gíve your stréngth to your sérvant
and sáve your hándmaid's són.   [repeat A]
17 Shów me a sígn of your fávour
that my fóes may sée to their sháme
that you consóle me and gíve me your hélp.

86

God's city, mother of all nations

*The universalist outlook here is truly astonishing: not that Zion ceases to
be the centre of the world—this in the psalmist's perspective will always
be so; but to offer the hand of friendship to Babylon and Egypt, the
ancient persecutors, is truly magnanimous. It may be, of course, that Jews
exiled in those countries are meant; but this would turn the wide and
gracious gesture of vv. 4-5 into something clumsy and ungenerous. With
this psalm may be compared a passage of the prophet Zechariah (8: 20-3;
cf. also 14: 16) where men from foreign countries 'take hold of the robe
of a Jew, saying: Let us go with you, for we have heard that God is with
you'. There is a Jew the whole world has heard of, and his surname is
Emmanuel, which means 'God with us'.*

1 On the hóly móuntain is his cíty
2 chérished by the Lórd.
  The Lórd prefers the gátes of Zíon
  to áll Jacob's dwéllings.
3 Of yóu are told glórious thíngs,
  O cíty of Gód!

4 'Bábylon and Égypt I will cóunt
  among thóse who knów me;
  Philístia, Týre, Ethiópia,
  thése will be her chíldren
5 and Zíon shall be cálled "Móther"
  for áll shall be her chíldren.'

  It is hé, the Lórd Most Hígh,
  who gives éach his pláce.
6 In his régister of péoples he wrítes:
  'Thése are her chíldren'
7 and whíle they dánce they will síng:
  'In yóu all find their hóme.'

87

Prayer in desolation

There is no sadness in any other psalm to be compared with this, and no psalm ends on such a note. One is so used to hearing the psalmist complain about his 'enemies' that when he does not, his silence is audible. There are no men complained of here—only God: but if he is an enemy, what hope is there? In this psalm there is no ray of light: it is a cry in the dark. The Dark is personified: it stands at his shoulder, and no one else stands there (v. 19) except the terrors of God (v. 18). The prayer of the psalmist is personified too: it knocks at God's door (v. 3) but even when it gains admission it obtains no audience (vv. 14-15). The inhuman enemy is sickness in a lonely old age: only God, whose messenger it is, can make the message bearable.

2 Lord my Gód, I call for hélp by dáy;
  I crý at níght befóre you.

3 Let my práyer cóme into your présence.
  O túrn your éar to my crý

4 For my sóul is fílled with évils;
  my lífe is on the brínk of the gráve.
5 I am réckoned as óne in the tómb:
  I have réached the énd of my stréngth,

6 like óne alóne among the déad;
  like the sláin lýing in their gráves;
  like thóse you remémber no móre,
  cut óff, as they áre, from your hánd.

7 You have láid me in the dépths of the tómb,
  in pláces that are dárk, in the dépths.
8 Your ánger weighs dówn upón me:
  I am drówned benéath your wáves.

9 You have táken awáy my fríends
  and máde me háteful in their síght.
  Imprísoned, I cánnot escápe;
10 my éyes are súnken with gríef.

  I cáll to you, Lórd, all the day lóng;
  to yóu I strétch out my hánds.
11 Will you wórk your wónders for the déad?
  Will the shádes stánd and práise you?

12 Will your lóve be tóld in the gráve
  or your fáithfulness amóng the déad?
13 Will your wónders be knówn in the dárk
  or your jústice in the lánd of oblívion?

14 As for mé, Lord, I cáll to you for hélp:
  in the mórning my práyer comes befóre you.
15 Lórd, why do you rejéct me?
  Whý do you híde your fáce?

16 Wrétched, close to déath from my yóuth,
  I have bórne your tríals; I am númb.
17 Your fúry has swépt down upón me;
  your térrors have útterly destróyed me.

18 They surróund me all the dáy like a flóod,
they assáil me áll togéther.
19 Friend and néighbour you have táken awáy:
my óne compánion is dárkness.

88

The magnificent promises of God

*Again, as in Psalm 79, the question 'why?'—but this time it is not so
much the disaster to the kingdom that worries the psalmist as the fate of
the Davidic King—perhaps the death at Megiddo of the devout Josiah in
609 B.C. and the extinction of the dynasty a few years later. If this in
fact was the occasion of the psalm we can only the more admire the faith of
the psalmist in such hard times. The messianic promise (2 Sam. 7) was
made by God, so were the heavens: each has the same guarantee: there is
no doubt about God's power and all kingship comes from him (vv. 6-19);
there is no doubt about God's promise either (vv. 20-38) so whatever has
happened (vv. 39-52) cannot be final. The psalmist was right: 'You
shall call his name Jesus . . . and the Lord God will give him the throne
of his father David . . . and of his kingdom there will be no end' (Lk.
1:31f).*

FORMULAS III 26
and II 24

2 I will síng for éver of your lóve, O Lórd;
through all áges my móuth will procláim your trúth.
3 Of thís I am súre, that your lóve lasts for éver,
that your trúth is fírmly estáblished as the héavens.

4 'With my chósen one Í have made a cóvenant;   [II 24]
I have swórn to Dávid my sérvant:
5 I will estáblish your dýnasty for éver
and sét up your thróne through all áges.'

6 The héavens procláim your wónders, O Lórd;   [III 26]
the assémbly of your hóly ones procláims your trúth.
7 For whó in the skíes can compáre with the Lórd
or whó is like the Lórd among the sóns of Gód?

158

8 A Gód to be féared in the cóuncil of the hóly ones,
  gréat and dréadful to áll aróund him.
9 O Lórd God of hósts, whó is your équal?
  You are míghty, O Lórd, and trúth is your gárment.

10 It is yóu who rúle the séa in its príde;
   it is yóu who stíll the súrging of its wáves.
11 It is yóu who trod Ráhab underfóot like a córpse,
   scáttering your fóes with your míghty árm.

12 The héavens are yóurs, the wórld is yóurs.
   It is yóu who fóunded the éarth and all it hólds;
13 it is yóu who creáted the Nórth and the Sóuth.
   Tábor and Hérmon shout with jóy at your náme.

14 Yóurs is a míghty árm, O Lórd;
   your hánd is stróng, your ríght hand réady.
15 Jústice and ríght are the píllars of your thróne,
   lóve and trúth wálk in your présence.

16 Háppy the péople who accláim such a kíng,
   who wálk, O Lórd, in the líght of your fáce,
17 who fínd their jóy every dáy in your náme,
   who máke your jústice the sóurce of their blíss.

18 For yóu, O Lórd, are the glóry of their stréngth;
   by your fávour it ís that our míght is exálted:
19 for our rúler ís in the kéeping of the Lórd;
   our kíng in the kéeping of the Hóly One of Ísrael.

*   *   *

20 Of óld you spóke in a vísion.   [II 24]
   To your fríends the próphets you saíd:
   'I have sét the crówn on a wárrior,
   I have exálted one chósen from the péople.

21 I have fóund Dávid my sérvant
   and with my hóly óil anóinted him.
22 My hánd shall álways be wíth him
   and my árm shall máke him stróng.

159

23 The énemy shall néver outwít him
nor the évil mán oppréss him.
24 I will béat down his fóes befóre him
and smíte thóse who háte him.

25 My trúth and my lóve shall be wíth him;
by my náme his míght shall be exálted.
26 I will strétch out his hánd to the Séa
and his ríght hand as fár as the Ríver.

27 He will sáy to me: "Yóu are my fáther,
my Gód, the róck who sáves me."
28 And I will máke hím my fírst-born,
the híghest of the kíngs of the éarth.

29 I will kéep my lóve for him álways;
with hím my cóvenant shall lást.
30 I will estáblish his dýnasty for éver,
make his thróne endúre as the héavens.

31 If his sóns forsáke my láw
and refúse to wálk as I decrée
32 and if éver they víolate my státutes,
refúsing to kéep my commánds;

33 then I will púnish their offénces with the ród,
then I will scóurge them on accóunt of their guílt
34 But I will néver take báck my lóve:
my trúth will néver fáil.

35 I will néver víolate my cóvenant
nor go báck on the wórd I have spóken.
36 Once for áll, I have swórn by my hóliness.
"I will néver líe to Dávid.
37 His dýnasty shall lást for éver.
In my síght his thróne is like the sún;
38 like the móon, it shall endúre for éver,
a fáithful wítness in the skíes." '

* * *

39 And yét you have spúrned, rejécted,
you are ángry with the óne you have anóinted.
40 You have bróken your cóvenant with your sérvant
and dishónoured his crówn in the dúst.

41 You have bróken down áll his wálls
and redúced his fórtresses to rúins.
42 He is despóiled by áll who pass bý:
he has becóme the táunt of his néighbours.

43 You have exálted the ríght hand of his fóes;
you have máde all his énemies rejóice.
44 You have máde his swórd give wáy,
you háve not uphéld him in báttle.

45 You have bróught his glóry to an énd;
you have húrled his thróne to the gróund.
46 You have cút short the yéars of his yóuth;
you have héaped disgráce upón him.

47 How lóng, O Lórd? Will you híde yourself for éver?

[VI 25]

How lóng will your ánger búrn like a fíre?
48 Remémber, Lórd, the shórtness of my lífe
and how fráil you have máde the sóns of mén.
49 What mán can líve and néver see déath?
Who can sáve himsélf from the grásp of the gráve?

50 Whére are your mércies of the pást, O Lórd,
whích you have swórn in your fáithfulness to Dávid?
51 Remémber, Lórd, how your sérvant is táunted,
how I háve to béar all the ínsults of the péoples.
52 Thús your énemies táunt me, O Lórd,
mócking your anóinted at évery stép.

*   *   *

53 Bléssed be the Lórd for ever. Amén, amén!

89

Pondering on the brevity of life

The plural pronouns no doubt indicate that this psalm was sung in community, but it scarcely reads like a national song and the application is surely to the congregation as individuals. The 'anger' and 'fury' of God (v. 11) have been used before (e.g. Psalm 6: 2) as a description of the brevity and the pain of life? It is always difficult to know how much the Christian's love of God owes to the revelation of a future life, but certainly he can admire those who loved God without it; as these grew older, one might have thought, their love of God would weaken in proportion since they had less to hope for. But instead it seemed to strengthen. Perhaps this is because the revelation was beginning to dawn already?

FORMULA V 9

1 O Lórd, you have béen our réfuge   [omit D]
from óne generátion to the néxt.
2 Befóre the móuntains were bórn
or the éarth or the wórld brought fórth,
you are Gód, without begínning or énd.

3 You túrn men báck into dúst
and say: 'Go báck, sóns of mén.'
4 To yóur eyes a thóusand yéars
are like yésterday, cóme and góne,
no móre than a wátch in the níght.

5 You swéep men awáy like a dréam,   [omit C+D]
like gráss which springs úp in the mórning.
6 In the mórning it springs úp and flówers:
by évening it wíthers and fádes.

7 So wé are destróyed in your ánger
strúck with térror in your fúry.
8 Our guílt lies ópen befóre you;
our sécrets in the líght of your fáce.

162

9 All our dáys pass awáy in your ánger.
Our lífe is óver like a sígh.
10 Our spán is séventy yéars
or éighty for thóse who are stróng.

And most of thése are émptiness and páin.
They pass swíftly and wé are góne.
11 Who understánds the pówer of your ánger
and féars the stréngth of your fúry?

12 Make us knów the shórtness of our lífe
that we may gáin wísdom of héart.
13 Lord, relént! Is your ánger for éver?
Show píty tó your sérvants.

14 In the mórning, fíll us with your lóve;
we shall exúlt and rejóice all our dáys.
15 Give us jóy to bálance our afflíction
for the yéars when we knéw misfórtune.

16 Show fórth your wórk to your sérvants;
let your glóry shíne on their chíldren.
17 Let the fávour of the Lórd be upón us:
give succéss to the wórk of our hánds
(give succéss to the wórk of our hánds).

90

Under the wing of God's protection

The devil can quote Scripture, and he quoted this (Mt. 4: 6): he was shrewd enough to recognise a quality and to try to play on its defects. But this is not quite accurate, because presumption is not a defect that corresponds to trust in God: the child who leaves his mother's hand to try his own two legs is not trusting her but himself. In any case, we must not let the devil spoil this psalm for us: for many people it is the most consoling in the psalter, and small wonder. It assures us in several quaintly assorted images that, no matter what the danger is, we have only to ask. The pathos of a God waiting—and longing—to be asked!

1 He who dwélls in the shélter of the Most Hígh
and abídes in the sháde of the Almíghty
2 sáys to the Lórd: 'My réfuge,
my strónghold, my Gód in whom I trúst!'

3 It is hé who will frée you from the snáre
of the fówler who séeks to destróy you;
4 hé will concéal you with his pínions
and únder his wíngs you will find réfuge.

5 You will not féar the térror of the níght
nor the árrow that flíes by dáy,
6 nor the plágue that prówls in the dárkness
nor the scóurge that lays wáste at nóon.

7 A thóusand may fáll at your síde,
tén thousand fáll at your ríght,
yóu, it will néver appróach;
*4c*his fáithfulness is. búckler and shíeld.

8 Your éyes have ónly to lóok
to sée how the wícked are repáid,
9 yóu who have said: 'Lórd, my réfuge!'
and have máde the Most Hígh your dwélling.

10 Upon yóu no évil shall fáll,
no plágue appróach where you dwéll.
11 For yóu has he commánded his ángels,
to kéep you in áll your wáys.

12 They shall béar you upón their hánds
lest you stríke your fóot against a stóne.
13 On the líon and the víper you will tréad
and trámple the young líon and the drágon.

14 Since he clíngs to me in lóve, I will frée him;
protéct him for he knóws my náme.
15 When he cálls I shall ánswer: 'I am wíth you.'
I will sáve him in distréss and give him glóry.

16 With léngth of life I will content him;
I shall lét him see my sáving pówer.

91

Song of a happy man

We are not animals, not even simply rational animals: we are sons of God; and we learn in prayer to look at the world as God sees it. We are joined to Christ as branches to the vine, and we try to make our minds, and our lives, grow more like his.

FORMULA V 55

2 It is góod to give thánks to the Lórd
to make músic to your náme, O Most Hígh,
3 to procláim your lóve in the mórning
and your trúth in the wátches of the níght,
4 on the tén-stringed lýre and the lúte,
with the múrmuring sóund of the hárp.

5 Your déeds, O Lórd, have made me glád;
for the wórk of your hánds I shout with jóy.
6 O Lórd, how gréat are your wórks!
How déep are yóur desígns!
7 The fóolish man cánnot knów this
and the fóol cánnot understánd.

8 Though the wícked spring úp like gráss
and áll who do évil thríve:
they are dóomed to be etérnally destróyed.
9 But yóu, Lord, are etérnally on hígh.
10 Sée how your énemies pérish;
all dóers of évil are scáttered.

11 To mé you give the wíld-ox's stréngth;
you anóint me with the púrest óil.
12 My éyes looked in tríumph on my fóes;
my éars heard gládly of their fáll.
13 The júst will flóurish like the pálm-tree
and grów like a Lébanon cédar.

14 Plánted in the hóuse of the Lórd
they will flóurish in the córts of our Gód,
15 stíll bearing frúit when they are óld,
stíll full of sáp, still gréen,
16 to procláim that the Lórd is júst,
In hím, my róck, there is no wróng.

92

Praise of God, king of the world

The first of the 'royal' psalms (92: 94-9) celebrating the kingship of God, creator and controller of our universe, whose eternal tranquillity contrasts with the restless sea. So calm he is and silent that we might think he sleeps. But only the God-made-man could sleep, and even then, when the apostles cried to him, 'He rebuked the wind and said to the sea: "Peace! Be still!" and the wind ceased and there was made a great calm' (Mk. 4: 39). 'You are a king then?' said Pilate. He is indeed—though his kingship was hidden. But now he sits at the right hand. Of his kingdom we are who is the image of the invisible God and in whom all things were created (Col. 1: 13ff). Let us sing to our Lord, ascended and throned in heaven.

FORMULA II 28

1 The Lord is kíng, with májesty enróbed;   [omit B]
the Lórd has róbed himself with míght,
he has gírded himsélf with pówer.

The wórld you made fírm, not to be móved;
2 your thróne has stood fírm from of óld.
From all etérnity, O Lórd, you áre.

3 The wáters have lífted up, O Lórd,
the wáters have lífted up their vóice,
the wáters have lífted up their thúnder.

4 Gréater than the róar of mighty wáters,
more glórious than the súrgings of the séa,
the Lórd is glórious on hígh.

166

5 Trúly your decrées are to be trústed.
Hóliness is fítting to your hóuse,
O Lórd, until the énd of tíme.

93

God, the judge and vindicator

*Is it all worth while, we must sometimes ask ourselves: religion doesn't
seem to make much difference, certainly doesn't seem to make us any
happier. But in spite of all difficulties we know that God does care. He
has redeemed us. And if we believe in redemption, then we must believe in
judgment. He cares for us, and he cares about us: what men do does
matter. But the difficulties are still there, and we need this vehement act of
faith in God who cares.*

FORMULA II 18

1 O Lórd, avénging Gód,
avénging Gód, appéar!
2 Júdge of the éarth, aríse,
gíve the próud what they desérve!

3 How lóng, O Lórd, shall the wícked,
how lóng shall the wícked tríumph?
4 They blúster with árrogant spéech;
the évil-doers bóast to each óther.

5 They crúsh your péople, Lórd,
they afflíct the ónes you have chósen.
6 They kíll the wídow and the stránger
and múrder the fátherless chíld.

7 And they sáy: 'The Lórd does not sée;
the God of Jácob páys no héed.'
8 Mark thís, most sénseless of péople;
fóols, when wíll you understánd?

9 Can hé who made the éar, not héar?
Can hé who formed the éye, not sée?

[v 17]

167

10 Will hé who trains nátions, not púnish?
Will hé who teaches mén, not have knówledge?
11 (The Lórd knows the thóughts of mén.
He knóws they are no móre than a bréath.)

12 Happy the mán whom you téach, O Lórd,   [ɪɪ 18]
whom you tráin by méans of your láw:
13 to hím you give péace in evil dáys
while the pít is being dúg for the wícked.

14 The Lórd will not abándon his péople
nor forsáke thóse who are his ówn:
15 for júdgment shall agáin be júst
and áll true héarts shall uphóld it.

16 Who will stánd up for mé against the wícked?
Who will defénd me from thóse who do évil?
17 If the Lórd were nót to hélp me,
I would sóon go dówn into the sílence.

18 When I thínk: 'I have lóst my fóothold';
your mércy, Lórd, holds me úp.
19 When cáres incréase in my héart
your consolátion cálms my sóul.

20 Can júdges who do évil be your fríends?
They do injústice under cóver of láw;
21 they attáck the lífe of the júst
and condémn ínnocent blóod.

22 As for mé, the Lórd will be a strónghold;
[v 17, omit ᴇ]
my Gód will be the róck where I take réfuge.
23 He will repáy them fór their wíckedness,
destróy them for their évil déeds.
The Lórd, our Gód, will destróy them.

168

94

Call to praise and worship:
a processional hymn

Over Israel God claimed a double kingship: she had been created and she had been chosen. Here she is invited (the psalm is called the 'Invitatorium') to celebrate both creation and choice. But she is warned, too. The flock divinely led from Egypt had disputed with Moses and tested God's patience by its complaints. It was at Raphidim in Sinai and so that place was called 'Massah and Meribah'—'Trial and Dispute' (cf. Exod. 17: 1-7). Now these things 'were written for our correction' (1 Cor. 10: 11); we may still thwart the grace of our call—it does not inevitably blossom into the glory of final choice. But how much higher than Israel's is our calling, and how much more sublime the election which, from man's point of view, we call perseverance! Not Moses but Jesus is our leader now, and the 'rest' he would take us to is not Palestine but a land which the meek inherit, a rest which is the eternal sabbath of God (Heb. 4: 10). Pray to hear not 'Never shall they enter!' but 'Come, ye blessed!'

FORMULA V 17

1 Come, ríng out our jóy to the Lórd;
   háil the róck who sáves us.
2 Let us cóme before him, gíving thánks,
   with sóngs let us háil the Lórd.

3 A míghty Gód is the Lórd,
   a gréat king abóve all góds.
4 In his hánd are the dépths of the éarth;
   the héights of the móuntains are hís.
5 To hím belongs the séa, for he máde it
   and the drý land sháped by his hánds.

6 Come ín; let us bów and bend lów;
   let us knéel before the Gód who máde us
7 for hé is our Gód and wé
   the péople who belóng to his pásture,
   the flóck that is léd by his hánd.

O that to-dáy you would lísten to his vóice!
8 'Hárden not your héarts as at Meríbah,
as on that dáy at Mássah in the désert
9 when your fáthers pút me to the tést;
when they tríed me, thóugh they saw my wórk.

10 For forty yéars I was wéaried of these péople
and I said: "Their héarts are astráy,
these péople do not knów my wáys."
11 Thén I took an óath in my ánger:
"Néver shall they énter my rést." '

95

The universal reign of the true God

*What can we bring to God, the Lord of the World? Before anything else
we bring him praise (v. 7), adoration, our delighted recognition of what
he is. 'Heaven and earth are full of his glory'; we proclaim the glory of
the Creator on behalf of all creation, and we wish our praise to resound
throughout the whole of creation.*

FORMULA II 1Ɛ

1 O síng a new sóng to the Lórd,
síng to the Lórd all the éarth.
2 O síng to the Lórd, bless his náme.

Procláim his hélp day by dáy,
3 téll among the nátions his glóry
and his wónders amóng all the péoples.

4 The Lord is gréat and wórthy of práise,
to be féared abóve all góds;
5 the góds of the héathens are náught.

It was the Lórd who máde the héavens,
6 his are májesty and státe and pówer
and spléndour in his hóly pláce.

170

7 Give the Lórd, you fámilies of péoples,
  give the Lórd glóry and pówer,
8 give the Lórd the glóry of his náme.

  Bring an óffering and énter his cóurts,
9 wórship the Lórd in his témple.
  O eárth, trémble befóre him.

10 Procláim to the nátions: 'God is kíng.'
  The wórld he made fírm in its pláce;
  he will júdge the péoples in fáirness.

11 Let the héavens rejóice and earth be glád,
  let the séa and all withín it thunder práise,
12 let the lánd and all it béars rejóice,
  all the trées of the wóod shout for jóy

13 at the présence of the Lórd for he cómes,
  he cómes to rúle the éarth.
  With jústice he will rúle the wórld,
  he will júdge the péoples with his trúth.

96

Earth rejoices in its king

The glory, the magnificence, the splendour of God—this could strike us with terror so that we might cry out like St. Peter, 'Depart from us!' But that glory is our light (v. 11); we are even called to share that glory. So for us, the majesty of God is not an object of terror, but a subject of exultation.

FORMULA II 28

1 The Lord is kíng, let éarth rejóice,
  let áll the cóastlands be glád.
2 Clóud and dárkness are his ráiment;
  his thróne, jústice and ríght.

3 A fíre prepáres his páth;
  it búrns up his fóes on every síde.

4 His líghtnings líght up the wórld,
the éarth trémbles at the síght.

5 The móuntains mélt like wáx
before the Lórd of áll the éarth.
6 The skíes procláim his jústice;
all péoples sée his glóry.

7 Let thóse who serve ídols be ashámed,   [omit B]
those who bóast of their wórthless góds.
All you spírits, wórship hím.

8 Zíon héars and is glád;
the péople of Júdah rejóice
becáuse of your júdgments O Lórd.

9 For yóu indéed are the Lórd
most hígh above áll the éarth
exálted far abóve all spírits.

10 The Lórd loves thóse who hate évil:
he guárds the sóuls of his sáints;
he séts them frée from the wícked.

11 Líght shines fórth for the júst
and jóy for the úpright of héart.
12 Rejóice, you júst, in the Lórd;
give glóry to his hóly náme.

97

Orchestra of praise to God, king of the world

Our Lord founded the kingdom of God on earth; and yet we pray, 'Thy kingdom come'; the work of our redemption has been accomplished, but we still pray for this salvation to be perfected throughout the world: God has come; but we look for his final coming, to take possession of his kingdom.

1 Síng a new sóng to the Lórd
for hé has worked wónders.
His ríght hand and his hóly árm
have bróught salvátion.

2 The Lórd has made knówn his salvátion;
has shown his jústice to the nátions.
3 He has remémbered his trúth and lóve
for the hóuse of Ísrael.

All the énds of the éarth have séen
the salvátion of our Gód.
4 Shóut to the Lórd all the éarth,
ríng out your jóy.

5 Sing psálms to the Lórd with the hárp
with the sóund of músic.
6 With trúmpets and the sóund of the hórn
acclaim the Kíng, the Lórd.

*　　*　　*

7 Let the séa and all withín it, thúnder;
the wórld, and all its péoples.
8 Let the rívers cláp their hánds
and the hílls ring out their jóy

9 at the présence of the Lórd: for he cómes,
he comes to rúle the éarth.
He will rúle the wórld with jústice
and the péoples with fáirness.

98

The power and holiness of God

*Our God is Almighty, infinitely above our world—but not remote from it.
On his word the world depends; his law is the rule of life. And the Church
is the place of contact between the Holy God and men called to be holy.*

1 The Lórd is kíng; the péoples trémble.
He is thróned on the chérubim; the eárth quákes.
2 The Lórd is gréat in Zíon.

Hé is supréme over áll the péoples.
3 Let them práise his náme, so térrible and gréat.
he is hóly, *4* fúll of pówer.

Yóu are a kíng who lóves what is ríght;
you have estáblished équity, jústice and ríght;
yóu have estáblished them in Jácob.

5 Exált the Lórd our Gód;
bow dówn before Zíon, his fóotstool.
Hé the Lórd is hóly.

6 Amóng his príests were Áaron and Móses,
among thóse who invóked his náme was Sámuel.
They invóked the Lórd and he ánswered.

7 To thém he spóke in the píllar of clóud.
They díd his wíll; they képt the láw,
which hé, the Lórd, had gíven.

8 O Lórd our Gód, you ánswered thém.
For thém yóu were a Gód who forgíves;
yet you púnished áll their offénces.

9 Exált the Lórd our Gód;
bow dówn before his hóly móuntain
for the Lórd our Gód is hóly.

99

Praise to God, creator and shepherd

The psalm bids us rejoice in God because we are utterly his. Its repetition is ecstatic: 'He made us; we belong to him; we are his people.' From God the relationship draws forth a steadfast love, for he cannot but love what is his own. From the psalmist the glad reflection provokes an outburst of gratitude. From those who know the Cross it should wring a cry of wonder that God should have bought what was already his own—that we should belong to him doubly. 'You are bought with a great price,' writes St. Paul; 'not with gold or silver,' Peter says, 'but with the precious blood of Christ' (1 Cor. 6: 20; 1 Pet. 1: 18). This psalm was born again on Calvary. We must remember that as we sing it.

FORMULA II 28

1 Cry out with jóy to the Lórd, all the éarth.   [omit B]
2 Sérve the Lórd with gládness.
Come befóre him, sínging for jóy.

3 Know that hé, the Lórd, is Gód.
He máde us, we belóng to hím,
we are his péople, the shéep of his flóck.

4 Gó within his gátes, giving thánks.
Enter his cóurts with sóngs of práise.
Give thánks to him and bléss his náme.

5 Indéed, how góod is the Lórd,
etérnal his mérciful lóve.
He is fáithful from áge to áge.

100

A pattern for rulers

This was the prayer of the king, who was responsible for the moral welfare of his people, as well as for their material well-being. Our Lord is the king of the Christian people: no sin was found in him, and he came to make it possible for all to share his own innocence. In union with him, we declare our resolution to spread the kingdom of justice and love—in our own hearts first.

FORMULA I 59

1 My sóng is of mércy and jústice;
I síng to you, O Lórd.
2 I will wálk in the wáy of perféction.
O whén, Lord, will you cóme?

175

I will wálk with blámeless héart
within my hóuse;
3 I will not sét befóre my éyes
whatéver is báse.

I will háte the wáys of the cróoked;
they sháll not be my fríends.
4 The false-héarted must kéep far awáy;
the wícked I disówn.

5 The man who slánders his néighbour in sécret
I will bríng to sílence.
The mán of proud lóoks and haughty héart
I will néver endúre.

6 I lóok to the fáithful in the lánd
that they may dwéll with mé.
He who wálks in the wáy of perféction
shall bé my fríend.

7 No mán who práctises decéit
shall líve within my hóuse.
No mán who utters líes shall stánd
befóre my éyes.

8 Mórning by mórning I will sílence
all the wícked in the lánd,
upróoting from the cíty of the Lórd
áll who do évil.

101

Prayer for renewal:
fifth psalm of repentance

This pathetic expression of grief suddenly changes (v. 13) into a confident
prayer for God's protection of Zion, his holy city. So we suffer with all
who suffer in the Church—while being certain that the gates of hell will
not prevail against it.

2 O Lórd, lísten to my práyer
and let my crý for hélp réach you.
3 Do not híde your fáce from mé
in the dáy of mý distréss.
Túrn your éar towárds me
and ánswer me quíckly when I cáll.

4 For my dáys are vánishing like smóke,
my bónes burn awáy like a fíre.
5 My héart is wíthered like the gráss.
I forgét to éat my bréad.
6 I crý with áll my stréngth
and my skín clíngs to my bónes.

7 I have becóme like a pélican in the wílderness,
like an ówl in désolate pláces.
8 I líe awáke and I móan
like some lónely bírd on a róof.
9 All day lóng my fóes revíle me;
those who háte me use my náme as a cúrse.

10 The bréad I éat is áshes;
my drínk is míngled with téars.
11 In your ánger, Lórd, and your fúry
you have lífted me up and thrówn me dówn.
12 My dáys are like a pássing shádow
and I wíther awáy like the gráss.

* * *

13 But ẏou, O Lórd, will endúre for éver*

[vi 25 and v 23]

and your náme from áge to áge.
14 Yóu will aríse and have mércy on Zíon:
for thís is the tíme to have mércy,
(yes, the tíme appóinted has cóme)
15 for your sérvants lóve her véry stónes,
are moved with píty éven for her dúst.

*The middle section has odd lines with 4 stresses and even lines
with 3. Sing odd lines to vi 25 and even to v 23.

177

16 The nátions shall féar the náme of the Lórd
and áll the earth's kíngs your glóry,
17 when the Lórd shall build up Zíon agáin
and appéar in áll his glóry.
18 Thén he will túrn to the práyers of the hélpless;
he will nót despíse their práyers.

19 Let thís be wrítten for áges to cóme
that a péople yet unbórn may praise the Lórd;
20 for the Lórd leaned dówn from his sánctuary on hígh.
He looked dówn from héaven to the éarth
21 that hé might héar the gróans of the prísoners
and frée those condémned to díe.

29 The sóns of your sérvants shall dwéll untróubled
and their ráce shall endúre befóre you
22 that the náme of the Lórd may be procláimed in Zíon
and his práise in the héart of Jerúsalem,
23 when péoples and kíngdoms are gáthered togéther
to páy their hómage to the Lórd.

* * *

24 He has bróken my stréngth in mid-cóurse;   [v 23]
he has shórtened the dáys of my lífe.
25 I say to Gód: 'Do not táke me awáy
befóre my dáys are compléte,
you, whose dáys last from áge to áge.

26 Long agó you fóunded the éarth
and the héavens are the wórk of your hánds.
27 They will pérish but yóu will remáin.
They will áll wear óut like a gárment.
You will chánge them like clóthes that are chánged.
28 But yóu neither chánge, nor have an énd.'

102

Praise of God's love

The Christian lives joyfully in the paradox that our God is higher than the heavens, and yet is close to us in love and mercy. Our gratitude for his mercy to us merges naturally into a hymn of praise for his greatness; and when we think how great he is, it is not to think how far away he is but how much he loves us to come down to us.

FORMULA V 30

1 My sóul, give thánks to the Lórd,
all my béing, bléss his holy náme.
2 My sóul, give thánks to the Lórd
and néver forgét all his bléssings.

3 It is hé who forgíves all your guílt,
who héals every óne of your ílls,
4 who redéems your lífe from the gráve,
who cRówns you with lóve and compássion,
5 who fílls your lífe with good thíngs,
renéwing your yóuth like an éagle's.

6 The Lórd does déeds of jústice,
gives júdgment for áll who are oppréssed.
7 He made knówn his wáys to Móses
and his déeds to Ísrael's sóns.

8 The Lórd is compássion and lóve,
slow to ánger and rích in mércy.
9 His wráth will cóme to an énd;
he will nót be ángry for éver.
10 He does not tréat us accórding to our síns
nor repáy us accórding to our fáults.

11 For as the héavens are hígh above the éarth
so stróng is his lóve for those who féar him.
12 As fár as the éast is from the wést
so fár does he remóve our síns.

13 As a fáther has compássion on his sóns,
    the Lord has píty on thóse who féar him;
14 for he knóws of whát we are máde,
    he remémbers that wé are dúst.

15 As for mán, his dáys are like gráss;
    he flówers like the flówer of the fíeld;
16 the wind blóws and hé is góne
    and his pláce never sées him agáin.

17 But the lóve of the Lórd is everlásting
    upon thóse who hóld him in féar;
    his jústice reaches óut to children's chíldren
18 when they kéep his cóvenant in trúth,
    when they kéep his wíll in their mínd.

19 The Lórd has set his swáy in héaven
    and his kíngdom is rúling over áll.
20 Give thánks to the Lórd, all his ángels,
    mighty in pówer, fulfílling his wórd,
    who héed the vóice of his wórd.

21 Give thánks to the Lórd, all his hósts,
    his sérvants who dó his wíll.
22 Give thánks to the Lórd, all his wórks,
    in évery pláce where he rúles.
    My sóul, give thánks to the Lórd!

103

God's boundless care for his creation: a psalm of worship

Religion is not a strictly private affair between God and our souls; we are part of a world, which God also made and loves. The creation was described in the first chapter of Genesis in brief phrases; here, the same account is painted in loving detail. The psalmist speaks of the world as he saw it; we can think also of the world as we know it—a much more complex world than the psalmist knew—but with the same delight and awe.

1 Bléss the Lórd, my sóul!
   Lord Gód, how gréat you áre,
   clóthed in májesty and glóry,
2 wrápped in líght as in a róbe!

*   *   *

   You strétch out the héavens like a tént.
3 Above the ráins you buíld your dwélling.
   You máke the clóuds your cháriot,
   you wálk on the wíngs of the wínd,
4 you máke the wínds your méssengers
   and fláshing fíre your sérvants.

5 You fóunded the éarth on its báse,
   to stand fírm from áge to áge.
6 You wrápped it with the ócean like a clóak:
   the wáters stood hígher than the móuntains.

7 At your thréat they tóok to flíght;
   at the vóice of your thúnder they fléd.
8 They róse over the móuntains and flowed dówn
   to the pláce which yóu had appóinted.
9 You set límits they míght not páss
   lest they retúrn to cóver the éarth.

10 You make spríngs gush fórth in the válleys:
   they flów in betwéen the hílls.
11 They give drínk to all the béasts of the fíeld;
   the wíld-asses quénch their thírst.
12 On their bánks dwell the bírds of héaven;
   from the bránches they síng their sóng.

13 From your dwélling you wáter the hílls;
   éarth drinks its fíll of your gíft.
14 You máke the grass grów for the cáttle
   and the plánts to sérve man's néeds,

   that he may bríng forth bréad from the éarth
15 and wíne to chéer man's héart;
   óil, to máke his face shíne
   and bréad to stréngthen man's héart.

181

16 The trées of the Lórd drink their fíll,
the cédars he plánted on Lébanon;
17 thére the bírds build their nésts:
on the trée-top the stórk has her hóme.
18 the góats find a hóme on the móuntains
and rábbits híde in the rócks.

19 You made the móon to márk the mónths;
the sún knows the tíme for its sétting.
20 When you spréad the dárkness it is níght
and all the béasts of the fórest creep fórth.
21 The young líons róar for their préy
and ásk their fóod from Gód.

22 At the rísing of the sún they steal awáy
and gó to rést in their déns.
23 Mán goes fórth to his wórk,
to lábour till évening fálls.

24 How mány are your wórks, O Lórd!   [omit B+C+E]
In wísdom you have máde them áll.
The éarth is fúll of your ríches.

25 Thére is the séa, vast and wíde,   [omit C]
with its móving swárms past cóunting,
líving things gréat and smáll.
26 The shíps are móving thére
and the mónsters you máde to pláy with.

27 Áll of thése look to yóu
to gíve them their fóod in due séason.
28 You gíve it, they gáther it úp:
you ópen your hánd, they have their fíll.

29 You híde your fáce, they are dismáyed;   [omit B]
you táke back your spírit, they díe,
retúrning to the dúst from which they cáme.
30 You sénd forth your spírit, they are creáted;
and you renéw the fáce of the éarth.

31 May the glóry of the Lórd last for éver!
May the Lórd rejóice in his wórks!

32 He lóoks on the éarth and it trémbles;
the móuntains send forth smóke at his tóuch.

33 I will síng to the Lórd all my lífe,
make músic to my Gód while I líve.
34 May my thóughts be pléasing to hím.
I fínd my jóy in the Lórd.
35 Let sínners vánish from the éarth
and the wícked exíst no móre.

Bléss the Lórd, my sóul.

104

God's faithfulness to his promise:
the story of Israel

We do not live in isolation from our material environment, nor do we from
our historical past, and the historical books of the Bible, like the Creation,
provide material for praise. The child is father of the man, and we are
what our past has made us. We are the people whom God has redeemed,
but in redeeming us God was keeping the promise which he made 'to our
fathers, to Abraham and to his seed'.

FORMULA II 51

Alleluia!

1 Give thánks to the Lórd, tell his náme,
make knówn his déeds among the péoples.

2 O síng to him, síng his práise;
téll all his wónderful wórks!
3 Be próud of his hóly náme,
let the héarts that seek the Lórd rejóice.

4 Consíder the Lórd and his stréngth;
cónstantly séek his fáce.
5 Remémber the wónders he has dóne,
his míracles, the júdgments he spóke.

6 O chíldren of Ábraham, his sérvant,
O sóns of the Jácob he chóse.
7 Hé, the Lórd, is our Gód:
his júdgments preváil in all the éarth.

8 He remémbers his cóvenant for éver,
his prómise for a thóusand generátions,
9 the cóvenant he máde with Ábraham,
the óath he swóre to Ísaac.

10 He confírmed it for Jácob as a láw,
for Ísrael as a cóvenant for éver.
11 He sáid: 'I am gíving you a lánd,
Cánaan, your appóinted héritage.'

12 Whén they were féw in númber,
a hándful of strángers in the lánd,
13 when they wándered from cóuntry to cóuntry,
from one kíngdom and nátion to anóther,

14 he allówed nó one to oppréss them;
he admónished kíngs on their accóunt:
15 'Do not tóuch thóse I have anóinted;
do no hárm to ány of my próphets.'

16 But he cálled down a fámine on the lánd;
he bróke the stáff that suppórted them.
17 He had sént a mán befóre them,
Jóseph, sóld as a sláve.

18 His féet were pút in cháins,
his néck was bóund with íron,
19 untíl what he sáid came to páss
and the wórd of the Lórd proved him trúe.

20 Then the kíng sént and reléased him;
the rúler of the péoples set him frée,
21 máking him máster of his hóuse
and rúler of áll he posséssed,

22 to instrúct his prínces as he pléased
and to téach his élders wísdom.
23 So Ísrael cáme into Égypt,
Jacob líved in the cóuntry of Hám.

24 He gáve his péople íncrease;
 he máde them strónger than their fóes,
25 whose héarts he túrned to hate his péople
 and to déal decéitfully with his sérvants.

26 Thén he sent Móses his sérvant
 and Áaron the mán he had chósen.
27 Through thém he shówed his márvels
 and his wónders in the cóuntry of Hám.

28 He sent dárkness, and dárk was máde
 but Égypt resísted his wórds.
29 He túrned the wáters into blóod
 and cáused their físh to díe.

30 Their lánd was alíve with frógs,
 éven in the hálls of their kíngs.
31 He spóke; the dóg-fly cáme
 and gnáts cóvered the lánd.

32 He sent háil-stones in pláce of the ráin
 and fláshing fíre in their lánd.
33 He strúck their vínes and fíg-trees;
 he sháttered the trées through their lánd.

34 He spóke; the lócusts cáme,
 young lócusts, too mány to be cóunted.
35 They áte up every bláde in the lánd;
 they áte up all the frúit of their fíelds.

36 He strúck all the fírst-born in their lánd,
 the fínest flówer of their sóns.
37 He led out Ísrael with sílver and góld.
 In his tríbes were nóne who fell behínd.

38 Égypt rejóiced when they léft
 for dréad had fállen upón them.
39 He spréad a clóud as a scréen
 and fíre to give líght in the dárkness.

40 When they ásked for fóod he sent quáils;
 he fílled them with bréad from héaven.
41 He píerced the róck to give them wáter;
 it gushed fórth in the désert like a ríver.

42 For he remémbered his hóly wórd,
which he gáve to Ábraham his sérvant.

43 So he bróught out his péople with jóy,
his chósen ones with shóuts of rejóicing.

44 And he gáve them the lánd of the nátions.
They tóok the frúit of óther men's tóil,

45 that thús they might kéep his précepts,
that thús they might obsérve his láws.

Alleluia!

105

Ingratitude of man:
the story of Israel

It is not only praise that the remembrance of our past calls forth: the story of the Old Testament is a story of man's sin and God's mercy, and 'Our sin is the sin of our fathers' (v. 6). We join with our fathers in confessing it. To have sinned is not fatal; but to fail to acknowledge it is—this cuts us off from the people of God, the people redeemed, the people of God's mercy.

FORMULA II 24

1 Alleluia!

O give thánks to the Lórd for he is góod;
for his lóve endúres for éver

2 Who can téll the Lórd's mighty déeds?
Whó can recóunt all his práise?

3 They are háppy who dó what is ríght,
who at áll times dó what is júst.

4 O Lórd, remémber mé
out of the lóve you háve for your péople.

Cóme to me, Lórd, with your hélp

5 that I may sée the jóy of your chósen ones
and may rejóice in the gládness of your nátion
and sháre the glóry of your péople.

186

6 Our sín is the sín of our fáthers;
  we have done wróng, our déeds have been évil.
7 Our fáthers when théy were in Égypt
  paid no héed to your wónderful déeds.

They forgót the gréatness of your lóve;
at the Réd Sea deféed the Most Hígh.
8 Yet he sáved them for the sáke of his náme,
  in órder to make knówn his pówer.

9 He thréatened the Red Séa; it dried úp
  and he léd them through the déep as through the désert.
10 He sáved them from the hánd of the fóe;
   he sáved them from the gríp of the énemy.

11 The wáters cóvered their oppréssors;
   not óne of them was léft alíve.
12 Thén they belíeved in his wórds:
   thén they sáng his práises.

13 But they sóon forgót his déeds
   and wóuld not wáit upon his wíll.
14 They yíelded to their crávings in the désert
   and put Gód to the tést in the wílderness.

15 He gránted them the fávour they ásked
   and sént diséase amóng them.
16 Then they rebélled, énvious of Móses
   and of Áaron, who was hóly to the Lórd.

17 The earth ópened and swállowed up Dáthan
   and búried the clán of Abíram.
18 Fíre blazed úp against their clán
   and flámes devóured the rébels.

19 They fáshioned a cálf at Hóreb
   and wórshipped an ímage of métal,
20 exchánging the Gód who was their glóry
   for the ímage of a búll that eats gráss.

21 They forgót the Gód who was their sáviour,
   who had dóne such great thíngs in Égypt,
22 such pórtents in the lánd of Hám,
   such márvels at the Réd Séa.

187

23 For thís he sáid he would destróy them,
but Móses, the mán he had chósen,
stóod in the bréach befóre him,
to túrn back his ánger from destrúction.

24 Then they scórned the lánd of prómise:
they hád no fáith in his wórd.
25 They compláined insíde their ténts
and would not lísten to the vóice of the Lórd.

26 So he ráised his hánd to swear an óath
that he would láy them lów in the désert;
27 would scátter their sóns among the nátions
and dispérse them throughóut the lánds.

28 They bówed before the Báal of Péor;
ate ófferings máde to lifeless góds.
29 They róused him to ánger with their déeds
and a plágue broke óut amóng them.

30 Then Phínehas stood úp and intervéned.
Thús the plágue was énded
31 and thís was cóunted in his fávour
from áge to áge for éver.

32 They provóked him at the wáters of Meríbah.
Through their fáult it went íll with Móses;
33 for they máde his héart grow bítter
and he úttered wórds that were rásh.

34 They fáiled to destróy the péoples
as the Lórd had gíven commánd,
35 but instéad they míngled with the nátions
and léarned to áct as théy did.

36 They wórshipped the ídols of the nátions
and thése became a snáre to entráp them.
37 They éven óffered their own sóns
and their dáughters in sácrifice to démons.

38 They shéd the blóod of the ínnocent,
the blóod of their sóns and dáughters
whom they óffered to the ídols of Cánaan.
The lánd was pollúted with blóod.

39 So they defíled themsélves by their déeds
and bróke their marriage bónd with the Lórd
40 till his ánger blázed against his péople:
he was fílled with hórror at his chósen ones.

41 So he gáve them into the hánd of the nátions
and their fóes becáme their rúlers.
42 Their énemies becáme their oppréssors;
they were subdúed benéath their hánd.

43 Tíme after tíme he réscued them,
but in their málice they dáred to défy him
and sank lów thróugh their guílt.
44 In spite of thís he paid héed to their distréss,
so óften as he héard their crý.

45 For théir sake he remémbered his cóvenant.
In the gréatness of his lóve he relénted
46 and he lét them be tréated with mércy
by áll who héld them cáptive.

47 O Lórd, our Gód, sáve us!
Bring us togéther from amóng the nátions
that we may thánk your hóly náme
and máke it our glóry to práise you.

*　　　*　　　*

48 Bléssed be the Lórd, God of Ísrael,
for éver, from áge to áge.
Let áll the péople cry óut:
'Amén! Amén! Allelúia!'

106

God's inexhaustible love

What we call 'redemption' comes to us in two stages—one already achieved, but the other not yet, not till the end of our lives. We are a pilgrim Church, and we still have to pass through the desert (v. 4), we are still in some degree bound by the chains of sin (v. 10), and we still have a stormy passage to make (v. 23). But the first stage of salvation is the guarantee of the second, and we pass through all this confident of God's protection (vv. 33ff).

1 'O give thánks to the Lórd for he is góod; [omit B+C]
for his lóve endúres for éver.'

2 Let them sáy this, the Lórd's redéemed,
whom he redéemed from the hánd of the fóe
3 and gáthered from fár-off lánds,
from éast and wést, north and sóuth.

       *   *   *

4 Some wándered in the désert, in the wílderness,
finding no wáy to a cíty they could dwéll in.
5 Húngry they wére and thírsty;
their sóul was fáinting withín them.

6 Then they críed to the Lórd in their néed
and he réscued thém from their distréss
7 and he léd them alóng the right wáy,
to reach a cíty théy could dwéll in.

8 Let them thánk the Lórd for his lóve,
for the wónders he dóes for mén.
9 For he sátisfies the thírsty sóul;
he fílls the húngry with good thíngs.

       *   *   *

10 Sóme lay in dárkness and in glóom,   [v 30]
prísoners in mísery and cháins,
11 having defíed the wórds of Gód
and spúrned the cóunsels of the Most Hígh.
12 He crúshed their spírit with tóil;
they stúmbled; there was nó one to hélp.

13 Then they críed to the Lórd in their néed   [II 31]
and he réscued thém from their distréss.
14 He led them fórth from dárkness and glóom
and bróke their cháins to píeces.

15 Let them thánk the Lórd for his góodness,
  for the wónders he dóes for mén:
16 for he búrsts the gátes of brónze
  and shátters the íron bárs.

        *   *   *

17 Some were síck on accóunt of their síns
  and afflícted on accóunt of their guílt.
18 They had a lóathing for évery fóod;
  they came clóse to the gátes of déath.

19 Then they críed to the Lórd in their néed
  and he réscued thém from their dístress.
20 He sént forth his wórd to héal them
  and sáved their lífe from the gráve.

21 Let them thánk the Lórd for his lóve,
  for the wónders he dóes for mén.
22 Let them óffer a sácrifice of thánks
  and téll of his déeds with rejóicing.

        *   *   *

23 Some sáiled to the séa in shíps
  to tráde on the míghty wáters.
24 Thése men have séen the Lord's déeds,
  the wónders he dóes in the déep.

25 For he spóke; he súmmoned the gále,
  tóssing the wáves of the séa
26 up to héaven and báck into the déep;
  their sóul melted awáy in their distréss.

27 They stággered, réeled like drunken mén,
  for áll their skíll was góne.
28 Then they críed to the Lórd in their néed
  and he réscued thém from their distréss.

29 He stílled the stórm to a whisper:
  all the wáves of the séa were húshed.
30 They rejóiced becáuse of the cálm
  and he léd them to the háven they desíred.

31 Let them thánk the Lórd for his lóve,
the wónders he dóes for mén.
32 Let them exált him in the gáthering of the péople
and práise him in the méeting of the élders.

* * *

33 He chánges stréams into a désert,
springs of wáter into thírsty gróund,
34 fruitful lánd into a sálty wáste,
for the wíckedness of thóse who líve there.

35 But he chánges désert into stréams,
thirsty gróund into spríngs of wáter.
36 Thére he séttles the húngry
and they buíld a cíty to dwéll in.

37 They sow fíelds and plánt their vínes;
thése yield cróps for the hárvest.
38 He blésses them; they grów in númbers.
He does not lét their hérds decréase.

* * *

40 He póurs contémpt upon prínces,
makes them wánder in tráckless wástes.
39 They dimínish, are redúced to nóthing
by oppréssion, évil and sórrow.

41 But he ráises the néedy from distréss;
makes fámilies númerous as a flóck.
42 The úpright sée it and rejóice
but áll who do wróng are sílenced.

43 Whoever is wíse, let him héed these thíngs
and consíder the lóve of the Lórd.

107

Prayer for victory

*God is lord of all men, not only of the Church; the People of God are at
his service—his helmet, his staff (v. 9)—in the task of making this lord-
ship an established fact. This is our responsibility, but also our joy and
confidence—not the wealth or wisdom or prestige of the Church, but simply
the fact that God is with us.*

FORMULA IV 5

2 My héart is réady, O Gód;　　　　　　　[omit B]
　　I will síng, síng your práise.
　　Awáke, my sóul;
3 awáke, lýre and hárp.
　　I will awáke the dáwn.

4 I will thánk you, Lórd, among the péoples,
　　among the nátions I will práise you,
5 for your lóve réaches to the héavens
　　and your trúth to the skíes.
6 O Gód, aríse above the héavens;
　　may your glóry shine on eárth!

7 O cóme and delíver your fríends;　　　[v 3, omit D]
　　hélp with your ríght hand and replý.
8 From his hóly place Gód has made this prómise:
　　'I will tríumph and divíde the land of Shéchem;
　　I will méasure out the válley of Súccoth.

9 Gílead is míne and Manásseh.　　　　　　[v 3]
　　Éphraim I táke for my hélmet,
　　Júdah for my commánder's stáff.
10 Móab I will úse for my wáshbowl,
　　on Édom I will plánt my shóe.
　　Over the Philistines I will shóut in tríumph.'

11 But who will léad me to cónquer the fórtress?
　　　　　　　　　　　　　　　　　[omit D+E]
　　Who will bríng me face to fáce with Édom?

12 Will you útterly rejéct us, O Gód,
   and no lónger márch with our ármies?

13 Give us hélp agáinst the fóe:
   for the hélp of mán is vaín.
14 With Gód wé shall do brávely
   and hé will trámple down our fóes.

See Psalm 59

108

Appeal for help against vicious enemies

*Christianity is not a milk-and-water philanthropy, and Christian charity
is not a vague benevolence. We have to love justice, and hate evil. And the
evil which we hate above all is lack of charity, the mark of the devil, the
enemy of man. This hatred calls for hatred (v. 17): we hate it wherever
it is found, and in ourselves first.*

FORMULA 1 6

1 O Gód whom I práise, do not be sílent: [omit B]
2 for the móuths of decéit and wíckedness
   are ópened agáinst me.

3 They spéak to me with lýing tóngues;   [omit B]
   they besét me with wórds of háte
   and attáck me without cáuse.

4 In retúrn for my lóve they accúse me
   while I práy for thém.
5 They repáy me évil for góod,
   hátred for lóve.

*   *   *

6 Appóint a wicked mán as his júdge: [II 4]
   let an accúser stánd at his ríght.
7 When he is júdged let him cóme out condémned;
   let his práyer be considered as sín.

194

8 Let the dáys of his lífe be féw;
   let anóther man táke his óffice.
 9 Let his chíldren be fátherless órphans
   and his wífe becóme a wídow.

10 Let his chíldren be wánderers and béggars
   dríven from the rúins of their hóme.
11 Let the créditor séize all his góods;
   let stróngers take the frúit of his wórk.

12 Let nó one shów him any mércy
   nor píty his fátherless chíldren.
13 Let áll his sóns be destróyed
   and wíth them their náme be blotted oút.

14 Let his fáther's guílt be remémbered,
   his móther's sín be retáined.
15 Let it álways stánd before the Lórd,
   that their mémory be cút off from the éarth.

16 For hé did not thínk of showing mércy   [v 3, omit D]
   but pursúed the póor and the néedy,
   hóunding the wrétched to déath.
17 He loved cúrsing; let cúrses fall upón him.
   He scorned bléssing; let bléssing pass him bý.

18 He pút on cúrsing like his cóat;
   let it sóak into his bódy like wáter;
   let it sínk like óil into his bónes;
19 let it bé like the clóthes that cóver him,
   like a gírdle he cánnot take óff!

                 *   *   *

20 Let the Lórd thus repáy my accúsers,   [omit D+E]
   all thóse who speak évil agáinst me.
21 For your náme's sake áct in my defénce;
   in the góodness of your lóve be my réscuer.

22 For Í am póor and néedy
   and my héart is píerced within me.
23 I fáde like an évening shádow;
   I am sháken óff like a lócust.

24 My knées are wéak from fásting;
  my bódy is thín and gáunt.
25 I have becóme an óbject of scórn,
  all who sée me tóss their héads.

26 Hélp me, Lórd my Gód;
  sáve me becáuse of your lóve.
27 Let them knów that thís is your wórk,
  that thís is your dóing, O Lórd.

28 They may cúrse but yóu will bléss.   [v 3, omit D]
  Let my attáckers be pút to sháme.
  but lét your sérvant rejóice.
29 Let my accúsers be clóthed with dishónour,
  cóvered with sháme ~as with~ a clóak.

30 Loud thánks to the Lórd are on my líps.
  I will praise him in the mídst of the thróng,
31 for he stánds at the póor man's síde
  to sáve him from thóse who condémn him.

109

The Messiah, king, priest and judge

Our Lord is the Son of God, begotten from eternity. As Son, he shares God's supreme dominion; but he exercises his power in priesthood; he does not want barren authority, but to gather all men to offer joyful homage in worship.

FORMULA PS 20

1 The Lórd's revelátion to my Máster:
  'Sít on my ríght:
  your fóes I will pút beneath your féet.'

2 The Lórd will wíeld from Zíon
  your scéptre of pówer:
  rúle in the mídst of all your fóes.

3 A prínce from the dáy of your bírth
on the hóly móuntains;
from the wómb before the dáwn I begót you.

4 The Lórd has sworn an óath he will not chánge.
'You are a príest for éver,
a príest like Melchízedek of óld.'

* * *

5 The Máster stánding at your ríght hand
will shatter kíngs in the dáy of his wráth.

6 Hé, the Júdge of the nátions,
will héap high the bódies;
héads shall be sháttered far and wíde.

7 He shall drínk from the stréam by the wáyside
and thérefore he shall líft up his héad.

I IO

The great works of God:
an alphabetical psalm

This is an alphabetic acrostic—each successive line begins with successive letters of the Hebrew alphabet. It is only to be expected that there is not much logical development of thought—it is more a series of separate reflections on the idea of reverence for God, awe, 'fear' (v. 10): but reverence for God who has saved us, bound himself to us in a covenant, and gives us food for soul and body.

FORMULA II 24

1 Alleluia!

I will thánk the Lórd with all my héart
in the méeting of the júst and their assémbly.
2 Gréat are the wórks of the Lórd;
to be póndered by áll who lóve them.

3 Majéstic and glórious his wórk,
his jústice stands fírm for éver.
4 He mákes us remémber his wónders.
The Lórd is compássion and lóve.

5 He gives fóod to thóse who féar him;
keeps his cóvenant éver in mínd.
6 He has shówn his míght to his péople
by gíving them the lánds of the nátions.

7 His wórks are jústice and trúth:
his précepts are áll of them súre,
8 standing fírm for éver and éver:
they are máde in úprightness and trúth.

9 He has sént delíverance to his péople   [omit B]
and estáblished his cóvenant for éver.
Hóly his náme, to be féared.

10 To fear the Lórd is the fírst stage of wísdom;   [omit B]
all who dó so próve themselves wíse.
His práise shall lást for éver!

I I I

The generous and upright man:
an alphabetical psalm

*Another alphabetic psalm, developing the thought of the last: the blessings
of salvation, and what our reverence for God involves in practice—mainly,
charity to our neighbour.*

FORMULA II 56

1 Alleluia!

Happy the mán who féars the Lórd,
who tákes delíght in all his commánds.
2 His sóns will be pówerful on éarth;
the children of the úpright are bléssed.

3 Ríches and wéalth are in his hóuse;
his jústice stands fírm for éver.
4 He is a líght in the dárkness for the úpright:
he is génerous, mérciful and júst.

5 The góod man takes píty and lénds,
he condúcts his affáirs with hónour.
6 The júst man will néver wáver:
hé will be remémbered for éver.

7 He has no féar of évil néws;
with a fírm heart he trústs in the Lórd.
8 With a stéadfast héart he will not féar;
he will sée the dównfall of his fóes.

9 Open-hánded, he gíves to the póor;
his jústice stands fírm for éver.
His héad will be ráised in glóry.

10 The wícked man sées and is ángry,
grinds his téeth and fádes awáy;
the desíre of the wícked leads to dóom.

112

*To the God of glory and compassion:
a psalm of worship*

To the Almighty Lord of heaven and earth praise is offered by us, his servants: but servants whom he also calls friends, raising us up to his own
height.

FORMULA V 17

1 Alleluia!

Práise, O sérvants of the Lórd,
práise the náme of the Lórd!
2 May the náme of the Lórd be bléssed
both nów and for évermóre!
3 From the rísing of the sún to its sétting
práised be the náme of the Lórd!

4 Hígh above all nátions is the Lórd,
abóve the héavens his glóry.
5 Whó is like the Lórd, our Gód,
who has rísen on hígh to his thróne
6 yet stóops from the héights to look dówn,
to look dówn upon héaven and éarth?

7 From the dúst he lífts up the lówly,
from the dúngheap he ráises the póor
8 to sét him in the cómpany of prínces,
yés, with the prínces of his péople.
9 To the chíldless wífe he gives a hóme
and gláddens her héart with chíldren.

113

The wonders of the Exodus: the one true God

*Our God is not a helpless idol; he is the living God—he is alive, in con-
stant activity; and it is the result of his action that we are alive as he is.
As if the river were to run backwards, as if the solid mountains were to
jump up and down—so astonishing is it that God should come to men to
make them share his life.*

FORMULA II 18

Alleluia!

When Ísrael came fórth from Égypt,
Jacob's sóns from an álien péople,
2 Júdah becáme the Lord's témple,
Ísrael becáme his kíngdom.

3 The séa fléd at the síght:
the Jórdan turned báck on its cóurse,
4 the móuntains léapt like ráms
and the hílls like yéarling shéep.

5 Whý was it, séa, that you fléd,
that you túrned back, Jórdan, on your cóurse?
6 Móuntains, that you léapt like ráms,
hílls, like yéarling shéep?

7 Trémble, O éarth, before the Lórd,
in the présence of the Gód of Jácob,
8 who túrns the róck into a póol
and flínt into a spríng of wáter.

(Psalm 115 in the Hebrew text)

1 Not to ús, Lórd, not to ús,
but to yóur náme give the glóry
for the sáke of your lóve and your trúth,
2 lest the héathen say: 'Whére is their Gód?'

3 But our Gód is ín the héavens;
he dóes whatéver he wílls.
4 Their ídols are sílver and góld,
the wórk of húman hánds.

5 They have móuths but they cánnot spéak;
they have éyes but they cánnot sée;
6 they have éars but they cánnot héar;
they have nóstrils but they cánnot sméll.

7 With their hánds they cánnot féel;
with their féet they cánnot wálk.
[No sóund cómes from their thróats.]
8 Their mákers will cóme to be líke them
and so will áll who trúst in thém.

9 Sons of Ísrael, trúst in the Lórd;
hé is their hélp and their shíeld.
10 Sons of Áaron, trúst in the Lórd;
hé is their hélp and their shíeld.

11 You who féar him, trúst in the Lórd;
hé is their hélp and their shíeld.
12 He remémbers us, and hé will bléss us;
he will bléss the sóns of Ísrael.
[He will bléss the sóns of Áaron.]

13 The Lord will bléss thóse who féar him,
the líttle no léss than the gréat:
14 to yoú may the Lórd grant íncrease,
to yóu and áll your chíldren.

15 May yóu be bléssed by the Lórd,
   the máker of héaven and éarth.
16 The héavens belóng to the Lórd
   but the éarth he has gíven to mén.

17 The déad shall not práise the Lórd,
   nor thóse who go dówn into the sílence.
18 But wé who líve bless the Lórd
   nów and for éver. Amén.

114

Prayer of a man saved from death

A simple prayer of thanks to God after escape from death by sickness, accident or malice. The psalm became part of the Hallel or 'Hymn of Praise' (Psalms 112-17) sung at the Paschal supper. Our Lord, therefore, went to death with the words on his lips. 'And a hymn being said, they went forth unto Mount Olivet.' But from him the words receive new life. Unlike the psalmist he does not ask to escape the snare of bodily death, rather he defies and defeats it: 'he could not be held by the bonds of death' (Acts 2: 24). The prayer of his human soul is for the glory of his risen body. With the psalmist we may recite the prayer after sickness, but with our Lord we may use it as gratefully on our deathbed, for 'he who raised Jesus Christ from the dead will raise us up also' (Rom. 8: 11).

FORMULA II I

1 Alleluia!

   I love the Lórd for hé has héard
   the crý of my appéal;
2 for he túrned his éar to mé
   in the dáy when I cálled him.

3 They surróunded me, the snáres of déath,
   with the ánguish of the tómb;
   they cáught me, sórrow and distréss.
4 I cálled on the Lórd's name.

   O Lórd my Gód, delíver me!

5 How grácious is the Lórd, and júst;
  our Gód has compássion.
6 The Lórd protécts the simple héarts;
  I was hélpless so he sáved me.

7 Turn báck, my sóul, to your rést
  for the Lórd has been góod;
8 he has képt my sóul from déath,
  (my éyes from téars)
  and my féet from stúmbling.

9 I will wálk in the présence of the Lórd
  in the lánd of the líving.

115

Promise in gratitude to God

The Hebrew text rightly makes this psalm one with the preceding. The theme remains the same but the psalmist now considers some outward expression of his gratitude. He can find nothing more noble than sacrifice; his 'cup of salvation' is the wine-libation that celebrates his temporal deliverance. How much more excellent is our salvation and how much worthier our cup! 'The chalice of benediction which we bless, is it not the communion of the blood of Christ?' (1 Cor. 10: 16). How could the Old Testament hope to make the thanks rival the gift? But now 'Where sin abounded grace more abounds' (Rom. 5: 20), and the sacrifice of the Son of God has no bounds. Through him our thanksgiving exceeds even the deliverance.

FORMULA II 1

10 I trústed, éven when I sáid:
  'I am sórely afflícted,'
11 and whén I sáid in my alárm:
  'No mán can be trústed.'

12 How cán I repáy the Lórd
  for his góodness to mé?
13 The cúp of salvátion I will ráise;
  I will cáll on the Lórd's name.

14 My vóws to the Lórd I will fulfíl
before all his péople.
15 O précious in the éyes of the Lórd
is the déath of his fáithful.

16 Your sérvant, Lord, your sérvant am Í;
you have lóosened my bónds.
17 A thánksgiving sácrifice I máke:
I will cáll on the Lórd's name.

18 My vóws to the Lórd I will fulfíl
before all his péople,
19 in the córts of the hóuse of the Lórd,
in your mídst, O Jerúsalem.

116

World-wide call to praise God

The knowledge of God's steadfast love for Israel must surely move hearts beyond her frontiers; the psalmist, therefore, invites all the world to join a choir of praise. His brief cry of joy rings above the Old Testament which so rarely sets the children of God's mercy side by side with the children of his promise. For this reason, the one who called himself the apostle of the Gentiles, triumphantly echoes the hymn which is their charter (Rom. 15: 11). You and I sing it often in the sacramental presence of him who died 'not only for the nation but to gather in one all the children of God' (Jn 11: 52). That presence, disdaining space and dissolving time, has carried the Holy of Holies outside its ancient borders. And now it is not Israel only but we of the nations who can sing, even more exultantly than the psalmist: 'Strong is his love for us.'

FORMULA PS 24

1 Alleluia!

O práise the Lórd, all you nátions,
accláim him all you péoples!

2 Stróng is his lóve for ús;
he is fáithful for éver.

117

Processional song of praise

'The stone which the builders rejected has become the corner stone' (v. 22) —so our Lord, rejected by his people and raised up by God; and so the Church, made up of those whom God has raised from death to life in union with the Risen Christ. The Church is the Temple of God, within which each of us sings our praise of God who has so loved us.

FORMULA IV 37

1 Alleluia!

Give thánks to the Lórd for he is góod,
for his lóve endures for éver.

✽ ✽ ✽

2 Let the sóns of Ísrael sáy:
'His lóve endures for éver.'
3 Let the sóns of Áaron sáy:
'His lóve endures for éver.'
4 Let thóse who fear the Lórd sáy:
'His lóve endures for éver.'

5 I cálled to the Lórd in my distréss;
he ánswered and fréed me.
6 The Lórd is at my síde; I do not féar.
What can mán do agáinst me?
7 The Lórd is at my síde as my hélper;
I shall look dówn on my fóes.

8 It is bétter to take réfuge in the Lórd   [omit ᴄ+ᴅ]
than to trúst in mén:
9 it is bétter to take réfuge in the Lórd
than to trúst in prínces.

10 The nátions áll encómpassed me;
in the Lórd's name I crúshed them.

205

11 They cómpassed me, cómpassed me abóut;
  in the Lórd's name I crúshed them.
12 They cómpassed me abóut like bées;
  they blázed like a fíre among thórns.   [repeat E]
  In the Lórd's name I crúshed them.

13 I was thrúst down, thrúst down and fálling
  but the Lórd was my hélper.
14 The Lórd is my stréngth and my sóng;
  hé was my sáviour.
15 There are shóuts of jóy and víctory
  in the ténts of the júst.

  The Lórd's right hánd has tríumphed;
16 his ríght hand ráised me.
  The Lórd's right hánd has tríumphed;
17 I shall not díe, I shall líve
  and recóunt his déeds.   [repeat D]
18 I was púnished, I was púnished by the Lórd,
  but nót doomed to díe.

19 Ópen to mé the gates of hóliness:
  I will énter and give thánks.
20 Thís is the Lórd's own gáte
  where the júst may énter.
21 I will thánk you for yóu have ánswered
  and yóu are my sáviour.

22 The stóne which the buílders rejécted
  has becóme the córner stone.
23 Thís is the wórk of the Lórd,
  a márvel in our éyes.
24 Thís day was máde by the Lórd;
  we rejóice and are glád.

25 O Lórd, gránt us salvátion;
  O Lórd, grant succéss.
26 Bléssed in the náme of the Lórd
  is hé who cómes.
  We bléss you from the hóuse of the Lórd;
27 the Lord Gód is our líght.

Go fórward in procéssion with bránches
éven to the áltar.
28 Yóu are my Gód, I thánk you.
My Gód, I práise you,
29 Give thánks to the Lórd for he is góod;
for his lóve endures for éver.

118

Love of God's law:
an alphabetical psalm

This is a long alphabetic psalm composed of stanzas of eight lines each, in which each verse begins with the same letter of the Hebrew alphabet. (Aleph, Beth, etc.). There is no logical development of thought, just a series of independent reflections, like ejaculations, meditating on various aspects of the same subject: the word of God, God's revelation of himself, which is also a revelation to us of the way we should live.

FORMULA PS 20

ALEPH

1 They are háppy whose life is blámeless,
who fóllow God's láw!
2 They are háppy who dó his wíll,
seeking hím with all their héarts,
3 who néver do ánything évil
but wálk in his wáys.
4 Yóu have laid dówn your précepts
to be obéyed with cáre.
5 Máy my fóotsteps be fírm
to obéy your státutes.
6 Thén I shall nót be put to sháme
as I héed your commánds.
7 I will thánk you with an úpright héart
as I léarn your decrées.
8 Í will obéy your státutes:
dó not forsáke me.

9 Hów shall the yóung remain sínless?
By obéying your wórd.
10 I have sóught you with áll my héart:
let me not stráy from your commánds.
11 I tréasure your prómise in my héart
lest I sín agáinst you.
12 Bléssed are yóu, O Lórd;
téach me your státutes.
13 With my tóngue I have recóunted
the decrées of your líps.
14 I rejóiced to dó your wíll
as though all ríches were míne.
15 I will pónder áll your précepts
and consíder your páths.
16 I táke delíght in your státutes;
I will nót forget your wórd.

GIMEL

17 Bless your sérvant and Í shall líve
and obéy your wórd.
18 Ópen my éyes that I may sée
the wónders of your láw.
19 Í am a pílgrim on the éarth;
shów me your commánds.
20 My sóul is éver consúmed
as I lóng for your decrées.
21 You thréaten the próud, the accúrsed,
who túrn from your commánds.
22 Relíeve me from scórn and contémpt
for I dó your wíll.
23 Though prínces sit plótting agáinst me
I pónder on your státutes.
24 Your wíll is mý delíght;
your státutes are my cóunsellors.

25 My sóul líes in the dúst;
    by your wórd revíve me.
26 I declåred my wåys and you ånswered:
    téach me your státutes.
27 Make me grásp the wáy of your précepts
    and I will múse on your wónders.
28 My sóul pines awáy with gríef;
    by your wórd raise me úp.
29 Kéep me from the wáy of érror
    and téach me your láw.
30 I have chósen the wáy of trúth
    with your decrées befóre me.
31 I bínd myself to dó your wíll;
    Lord, dó not disappóint me.
32 I will rún the wáy of your commánds;
    you give fréedom to my héart.

HE

33 Téach me the demánds of your státutes
    and I will kéep them to the énd.
34 Tráin me to obsérve your láw,
    to kéep it with my héart.
35 Guíde me in the páth of your commánds;
    for thére is my delíght.
36 Bénd my héart to your wíll
    and nót to love of gáin.
37 Kéep my éyes from what is fálse:
    by your wórd, give me lífe.
38 Kéep the prómise you have máde
    to the sérvant who féars you.
39 Kéep me from the scórn I dréad,
    for your decrées are góod.
40 Sée, I lóng for your précepts:
    then in your jústice, give me lífe.

VAU

41 Lórd, let your lóve come upón me,
the saving hélp of your prómise.

42 And I shall ánswer thóse who táunt me
for I trúst in your wórd.

43 Do not táke the word of trúth from my móuth
for I trúst in your decrées.

44 I shall álways kéep your láw
for éver and éver.

45 I shall wálk in the páth of fréedom
for I séek your précepts.

46 I will spéak of your wíll before kíngs
and nót be abáshed.

47 Your commánds have béen my delíght;
thése I have lóved.

48 I will wórship your commánds and lóve them
and pónder your státutes.

ZAYIN

49 Remémber your wórd to your sérvant
by whích you gave me hópe.

50 Thís is my cómfort in sórrow
that your prómise gives me lífe.

51 Though the próud may útterly deríde me
I kéep to your láw.

52 I remémber your decrées of óld
and thése, Lord, consóle me.

53 I am séized with indignátion at the wícked
who forsáke your láw.

54 Your státutes have becóme my sóng
in the lánd of éxile.

55 I thínk of your náme in the níght-time
and I kéep your láw.

56 Thís has béen my bléssing,
the kéeping of your précepts.

HETH

57 My párt, I have resólved, O Lórd,
   is to obéy your wórd.
58 With all my héart I implóre your fávour;
   show the mércy of your prómise.
59 I have póndered óver my wáys
   and retúrned to your wíll.
60 I made háste and díd not deláy
   to obéy your commánds.
61 Though the néts of the wícked ensnáred me
   I remémbered your láw.
62 At mídnight I will ríse and thánk you
   for your júst decrées.
63 I am a fríend of áll who revére you,
   who obéy your précepts.
64 Lórd, your lóve fills the éarth.
   Téach me your státutes.

TETH

65 Lórd, you have been góod to your sérvant
   accórding to your wórd.
66 Téach me discérnment and knówledge
   for I trúst in your commánds.
67 Befóre I was afflícted I stráyed
   but nów I keep your wórd.
68 You are góod and your déeds are góod;
   téach me your státutes.
69 Though próud men sméar me with líes
   yet I kéep your précepts.
70 Their mínds are clósed to góod
   but your láw is my delíght.
71 It was góod for mé to be afflícted,
   to léarn your státutes.
72 The láw from your móuth means móre to me
   than sílver and góld.

73 It was yóur hands that máde me and sháped me:
help me to léarn your commánds.

74 Your fáithful will sée me and rejóice
for I trúst in your wórd.

75 Lord, I knów that your decrées are ríght,
that you afflícted me jústly.

76 Let your lóve be réady to consóle me
by your prómise to your sérvant.

77 Let your lóve cóme and I shall líve
for your láw is my delíght.

78 Shame the próud who hárm me with líes
while I pónder your précepts.

79 Let your fáithful túrn to mé,
those who knów your wíll.

80 Let my héart be blámeless in your státutes
lést I be ashámed.

81 I yéarn for your sáving hélp;
I hópe in your wórd.

82 My éyes yéarn to see your prómise.
Whén will you consóle me?

83 Though párched and exháusted with wáiting
I remémber your státutes.

84 How lóng must your sérvant súffer?
When will you júdge my fóes?

85 For mé the próud have dug pítfalls,
agáinst your láw.

86 Your commánds are all trúe; then hélp me
when líes oppréss me.

87 They álmost made an énd of me on éarth
but I képt your précepts.

88 Becáuse of your lóve give me lífe
and Í will do your wíll.

89 Your wórd, O Lórd, for éver
   stands fírm in the héavens:
90 your trúth lasts from áge to áge,
   like the éarth you creáted.
91 By your decrée it endúres to this dáy;
   for áll things sérve you.
92 Had your láw not béen my delíght
   I would have díed in my afflíction.
93 I will néver forgét your précepts
   for with thém you give me lífe.
94 Sáve me, for Í am yoúrs
   since I séek your précepts.
95 Though the wícked lie in wáit to destróy me
   yet I pónder on your wíll.
96 I have séen that all perféction has an énd
   but your commánd is bóundless.

97 Lórd, how I lóve your láw!
   It is éver in my mínd.
98 Your commánd makes me wíser than my fóes;
   for it is míne for éver.
99 I have more ínsight than áll who téach me
   for I pónder your wíll.
100 I have móre understánding than the óld
    for I kéep your précepts.
101 I turn my féet from évil páths
    to obéy your wórd.
102 I háve not túrned from your decrées;
    you yoursélf have táught me.
103 Your prómise is swéeter to my táste
    than hóney in the móuth.
104 I gáin understánding from your précepts
    and so I háte false wáys.

105 Your wórd is a lámp for my stéps
    and a líght for my páth.
106 I have swórn and have máde up my mínd
    to obéy your decrées.
107 Lórd, I am déeply afflícted:
    by your wórd give me lífe.
108 Accépt, Lord, the hómage of my líps
    and téach me your decrées.
109 Though I cárry my lífe in my hánds,
    I remémber your láw.
110 Though the wícked trý to ensnáre me
    I do not stráy from your précepts.
111 Your wíll is my héritage for éver,
    the jóy of my héart.
112 I sét myself to cárry out your státutes
    in fúllness, for éver.

SAMECH

113 I have no lóve for hálf-hearted mén;
    my lóve is for your láw.
114 Yóu are my shélter, my shíeld;
    I hópe in your wórd.
115 Léave me, yóu who do évil;
    I will kéep God's commánd.
116 If you uphóld me by your prómise I shall líve;
    let my hópes not be in váin.
117 Sustáin me and Í shall be sáved
    and ever obsérve your státutes.
118 You spúrn all who swérve from your státutes;
    their cúnning is in váin.
119 You thrów away the wícked like dróss;
    so I lóve your wíll.
120 I trémble befóre you in térror;
    I féar your decrées.

121 I have dóne what is ríght and júst:
let me nót be oppréssed.

122 Vóuch for the wélfare of your sérvant
lest the próud oppréss me.

123 My eyes yéarn for your sáving hélp
and the prómise of your jústice.

124 Tréat your sérvant with lóve
and téach me your státutes.

125 Í am your sérvant, give me knówledge;
then I shall knów your wíll.

126 It is tíme for the Lórd to áct
for your láw has been bróken.

127 Thát is why I lóve your commánds
more than fínest góld,

128 why I rúle my lífe by your précepts:
and háte false wáys.

PE

129 Your wíll is wónderful indéed;
thérefore I obéy it.

130 The unfólding of your wórd gives líght
and téaches the símple.

131 I ópen my móuth and I sígh
as I yéarn for your commánds.

132 Túrn and shów me your mércy;
show jústice to your fríends.

133 Let my stéps be guíded by your prómise;
let no évil rúle me.

134 Redéem me from mán's oppréssion
and Í will keep your précepts.

135 Let your fáce shíne on your sérvant
and téach me your decrées.

136 Téars stréam from my éyes
because your láw is disobéyed.

137 Lórd, you are júst indéed;
   your decrées are ríght.
138 You have impósed your will with jústice
   and with ábsolute trúth.
139 I am cárried awáy by ánger
   for my fóes forget your wórd.
140 Your prómise is tríed in the fíre,
   the delíght of your sérvant.
141 Althóugh I am wéak and despísed
   I remémber your précepts.
142 Your jústice is etérnal jústice
   and your láw is trúth.
143 Though ánguish and distréss have séized me,
   I delíght in your commánds.
144 The jústice of your will is etérnal:
   if you téach me, I shall líve.

KOPH

145 I cáll with all my héart; Lord, héar me,
   I will kéep your státutes.
146 I cáll upón you, sáve me
   and Í will do your will.
147 I ríse before dáwn and cry for hélp,
   I hópe in your wórd.
148 My éyes wátch through the níght
   to pónder your prómise.
149 In your lóve hear my vóice, O Lórd;
   give me lífe by your decrées.
150 Those who hárm me unjústly draw néar:
   they are fár from your láw.
151 But yóu, O Lórd, are clóse:
   your commánds are trúth.
152 Lóng have I knówn that your will
   is estáblished for éver.

153 Sée my afflíction and sáve me
for I remémber your láw.

154 Uphóld my cáuse and defénd me;
by your prómise, give me lífe.

155 Salvátion is fár from the wícked
who are héedless of your státutes.

156 Númberless, Lórd, are your mércies;
with your decrées give me lífe.

157 Though my fóes and oppréssors are cóuntless
I have not swérved from your wíll.

158 I lóok at the fáithless with disgúst;
they ignóre your prómise.

159 Sée how I lóve your précepts;
in your mércy give me lífe.

160 Your wórd is fóunded on trúth:
your decrées are etérnal.

SHIN

161 Though prínces oppréss me without cáuse
I stand in áwe of your wórd.

162 I táke delight in your prómise
like óne who finds a tréasure.

163 Líes I háte and detést
but your láw is my lóve.

164 Séven times a dáy I práise you
for your júst decrées.

165 The lóvers of your láw have great péace;
they néver stúmble.

166 I awáit your saving hélp, O Lórd,
I fulfíl your commánds.

167 My sóul obéys your wíll
and lóves it déarly.

168 I obéy your précepts and your wíll;
all that I dó is befóre you.

169 Lórd, let my crý come befóre you:
téach me by your wórd.

170 Let my pléading cóme befóre you;
sáve me by your prómise.

171 Let my líps procláim your práise
because you téach me your státutes.

172 Let my tóngue síng your prómise
for your commánds are júst.

173 Let your hánd be réady to hélp me,
since I have chósen your précepts.

174 Lord, I lóng for your sáving hélp
and your láw is my delíght.

175 Give lífe to my sóul that I may práise you.
Let your decrées give me hélp.

176 I am lóst like a shéep; seek your sérvant
for I remémber your commánds.

119

Amongst treacherous strangers: a pilgrimage song

First of the 'Psalms of Ascent' (Psalms 119-33) sung by pilgrims journey-ing to the holy hill of Zion. Compared with this sacred ground the whole world is barbarous: the exile feels himself in Meshech (in the Caucasus, Gen. 10: 2) or amongst the fierce tribes of the Arabian deserts (Kedar, Gen. 25: 13). God will judge the lying mouths and hostile intents that surround him. But the psalm must be transposed to the Christian key: the spirit of the New Testament is of another sort. 'Pray for them that calumniate you' is our Lord's instruction (Mt. 5: 43ff). We acknowledge no enemy but of the soul. We pray that God will rain down his destroying judgments upon our enemy within, deceitful, treacherous, waging constant war. We pray against our own selfish selves.

1 To the Lórd in the hóur of my distréss
I cáll and he ánswers me.
2 'O Lórd, save my sóul from lying líps,
from the tóngue of the decéitful.'

3 Whát shall he páy you in retúrn,
O tréacherous tóngue?
4 The wárrior's árrows shárpened
and cóals, red-hot, blázing.

[*5* Alas, that I abíde a stránger in Méshech,
dwell among the ténts of Kédar!]

6 Long enóugh have Í been dwélling
with thóse who hate péace.
7 Í am for péace, but when I spéak,
théy are for fíghting.

1 20

God the protector:
a pilgrimage song

The pilgrim lifts his face towards the temple on the height of Zion. It is the earthly home of the one God, tireless guardian of Israel. We, too, journey 'to Mount Zion, the city of the living God, the heavenly Jerusalem' with which the old Jerusalem of stone cannot compare. 'We have here no lasting city; we seek the city that is to come' (Heb. 13: 14). And in that city there is one who prays: 'Now I am not in the world and these are in the world. Holy Father . . . I pray not that thou shouldst take them out of the world but that thou shouldst keep them from evil' (Jn 17: 11, 15). To that height and so to that shrine we confidently lift our eyes and sing our prayer.

1 I lift up my éyes to the móuntains:
from whére shall come my hélp?
2 My hélp shall cóme from the Lórd
who made héaven and éarth.

3 May he néver állow you to stúmble!
Let him sléep not, your guárd.
4 Nó, he sléeps not nor slúmbers,
Ísrael's guárd.

5 The Lórd is your guárd and your sháde;
at your ríght side he stánds.
6 By dáy the sún shall not smíte you
nor the móon in the níght.

7 The Lórd will guárd you from évil,
he will guárd your sóul.
8 The Lord will guárd your góing and cóming
both nów and for éver.

121

Greeting to Jerusalem:
a pilgrimage song

*Joy of the pilgrim who reaches his goal at last—Jerusalem, elected home
of God, venerable in the tradition of Israel. Here is a deep sense of home-
coming and of pride in that home. We of the world-wide 'Israel of God'
have no city to house us all; we are 'of the household of the faith' (Gal.
6: 10). But we have the brothers and sisters whom Jesus promised to
those of his company (Mk 9: 30); we have a home which we call 'the
Church'. It stands scarred with years of siege but, by God's grace, compact
and dignified by the marks of its resistance. We may take pride in it
because the strength of its walls is from God. It will never have peace
from without; let us pray and work for its peace within, which is 'the
love of brethren'.*

FORMULA I 15

1 I rejóiced when I héard them sáy:
'Let us gó to God's hóuse.'
2 And nów our féet are stánding
within your gátes, O Jerúsalem.

3 Jerúsalem is buílt as a cíty
stróngly compáct.

4 It is thére that the tríbes go úp,
the tríbes of the Lórd.

For Ísrael's láw it ís,
there to práise the Lord's náme.
5 Thére were set the thrónes of júdgment
of the hóuse of Dávid.

6 For the péace of Jerúsalem práy:
'Péace be to your hómes!
7 May péace réign in your wálls,
in your pálaces, péace!'

8 For lóve of my bréthren and fríends
I say: 'Péace upon yóu!'
9 For lóve of the hóuse of the Lórd
I will ásk for your góod.

I22

Cry for help:
a pilgrimage song

The exiles returned from Babylon to a ruined city and a neglected land. Hostile colonists mocked their efforts to rebuild (Neh. 2: 19). This short hymn expresses the trust that upheld this 'remnant of Israel'. The mute appeal of the 'eyes' marks the simplicity of the psalm. It is so simple, indeed, that it would scarcely seem to need adapting to the true Christian heart. Yet here, as everywhere, the Incarnation has worked its miracle. For the psalmist the Lord is lord and he the slave, but the Son has made us free (Jn 8: 36) and St. Paul joyfully cries: 'No more a slave but a son!' (Gal. 4: 7). The eyes that we turn to God are the eyes of a child sure that it is loved, they are not the eyes of an anxious servant. Bidding us say: 'Father!' our Lord would have us think of ourselves as children. Let me sing this psalm like a child.

FORMULA I 52

1 To ýou have I lífted up my éyes,
you who dwéll in the héavens:
2 my éyes, like the éyes of sláves
on the hánd of their lórds.

Líke the éyes of a sérvant
on the hánd of her místress,
3 so our éyes are on the Lórd our Gód
till he shów us his mércy.

4 Have mércy on us, Lórd, have mércy.
We are fílled with contémpt.
5 Indéed all too fúll is our sóul
with the scórn of the rích,
(with the próud man's disdáin).   [re̜peat D]

123

Thanksgiving for help in crisis:
a pilgrimage song

Our adversary the devil goes round like a roaring lion: like a man swept
away by a flood, like a bird caught in a trap, how helpless we are, how
lost—except for God.

FORMULA I 15

1 'If the Lórd had not béen on our síde,'
this is Ísrael's sóng.   [repeat A+B]
2 'If the Lórd had not béen on our síde
when mén rose agáinst us,
3 thén would they have swállowed us alíve
when their ánger was kíndled.

4 Thén would the wáters have engúlfed us,
the tórrent gone óver us;
5 óver our héad would have swépt
the ráging wáters.'

6 Bléssed be the Lórd who did not gíve us
a préy to their téeth!
7 Our lífe, like a bírd, has escáped
from the snáre of the fówler.

222

Indéed the snáre has been bróken
and wé have escáped.
8 Our hélp is in the náme of the Lórd,
who made héaven and éarth.

124

Unshakable faith:
a pilgrimage song

The Church is built on a rock—rock-based and rock-girt. Our faith will
be tested, but to leave this fortress is to abandon our only hope.

FORMULA I 6

1 Thóse who put their trúst in the Lórd   [omit B]
are like Mount Zíon, that cánnot be sháken,
that stánds for éver.

2 Jerúsalem! The móuntains surróund her,   [omit B]
so the Lórd surróunds his péople
both nów and for éver.

3 For the scéptre of the wícked shall not rést
over the lánd of the júst
for féar that the hánds of the júst
should túrn to évil.

4 Do góod, Lord, to thóse who are góod,
to the úpright of héart;
5 but the cróoked and thóse who do évil,
dríve them awáy!

On Ísrael, péace!

125

Song of the returned exiles:
a pilgrimage song

Joy after the sorrows of exile (vv. 1-2) is an earnest of new joy to come after the first disappointments of return (vv. 3-4). Israel's drought will turn to fertility; her long labour of sowing will achieve its harvest. How bitter the sowing was to be the psalmist could not know, nor how great the harvest. 'The field is the world' (Mt. 13: 38) and the field whitens for a harvest of souls gathered to eternal life (Jn 4: 35ff; Mt. 13: 30). But the sowing is in tears: 'Unless the seed falls into the ground and dies, it remains alone' (Jn 12: 24ff). The seed is the Word—the Word made flesh and crucified. The tears are his, the joy ours: 'What marvels the Lord worked for us!' And yet we, too, have our crucifixion. St. Paul's assurance should make us brave: 'We sow a corruptible body to rise imperishable' (1 Cor. 15: 43). The Old Testament hope was only a shadow of ours.

FORMULA I 15

1 When the Lórd delivered Zíon from bóndage,
  It séemed like a dréam.
2 Thén was our móuth filled with láughter,
  on our líps there were sóngs.

  The héathens themsélves said: 'What márvels
  the Lórd worked for thém!'
3 What márvels the Lórd worked for ús!
  Indéed we were glád.

4 Delíver us, O Lórd, from our bóndage
  as stréams in dry lánd.
5 Thóse who are sówing in téars
  will síng when they réap.

6 They go óut, they go óut, full of téars,
  carrying séed for the sówing:
  they come báck, they come báck, full of sóng,
  cárrying their shéaves.

126

Success depends on God's blessing: a pilgrimage song

Human anxiety offers an insult to God—and it is futile. House, food, family are all from God. Without him man is homeless, starving, barren. 'Be not anxious, your Father knows you need all these things' (Mt. 6: 25ff). Such earthly gifts, implicit objects of the psalmist's prayer, are the frontier of his ambition. This Old Testament expression of trust will never lose its worth but the ambition of the New ranges wider and higher. The Christian mind must dwell less on gift than on grace. The house he builds, the city he guards (not he but the Lord) is his own soul, home and shrine of the Trinity (2 Cor. 6: 16). The bread he asks is not only his daily bread but the bread the Son of Man will give (Jn 6: 27). The children his heart would bring forth through the overshadowing Spirit are Charity, Joy, Peace. Happy the man whose quiver God fills with these! Ask and you shall receive.

FORMULA II 28

1 If the Lórd does not buíld the hóuse,
   in váin do its buílders lábour;
   if the Lórd does not wátch over the cíty,
   in váin does the wátchman keep vígil.

2 In váin is your éarlier rísing,
   your góing láter to rést,
   you who tóil for the bréad you éat:
   when he pours gífts on his belóved while they slúmber.

3 Truly sóns are a gíft from the Lórd,
   a bléssing, the frúit of the wómb.
4 Indéed the sóns of yóuth
   are like árrows in the hánd of a wárrior.

5 Ó the háppiness of the mán
   who has fílled his quíver with these árrows!
   Hé will have no cáuse for sháme
   when he dispútes with his fóes in the gáteways.

127

The blessings of home:
a pilgrimage song

A fellow to the previous psalm, developing the idea of its second part. With sound instinct it asks God for a Jerusalem of godfearing, happy homes. Men and women have their own part in building it—in our psalm complements its predecessor's emphasis upon God's prevailing work. But what is Jerusalem to us? The new Jerusalem for which we pray is 'the Church of the firstborn' (Heb. 12: 23), the heaven on earth of which every Christian is citizen (cf. Phip. 1: 27, 3: 30; Eph. 2: 19). In her the promises of the Old Testament are fulfilled and its prayers made sublime: it is around 'the table of the Lord' that the Spouse of Christ seats her ever-growing family (1 Cor. 10: 21; Eph. 5: 32). Pray God for the happiness and peace of this family.

FORMULA IV 58

1 O bléssed are thóse who fear the Lórd
and wálk in his wáys!

2 By the lábour of your hánds you shall éat.
You will be háppy and prósper;
3 your wífe like a frúitful víne
in the héart of your hóuse;
your chíldren like shóots of the ólive,
aróund your táble.

4 Indéed thús shall be bléssed
the mán who fears the Lórd.
5 May the Lórd bléss you from Zíon
5c all the dáys of your lífe!
6 May you sée your chíldren's chíldren
5b in a háppy Jerúsalem!

On Ísrael, péace!

128

The fate of Israel's enemies:
a pilgrimage song

A field of ripe corn, a rich harvest—this is a good picture of God's bounty to us: but the harvest is brought forth after painful ploughing.

FORMULA I 15

1 'They have préssed me hárd from my yóuth,'
this is Ísrael's sóng.
2 'They have préssed me hárd from my yóuth
but could néver destróy me.

3 They plóughed my báck like plóughmen,
drawing lóng fúrrows.
4 But the lórd who is júst, has destróyed
the yóke of the wícked.'

5 Lét them be shámed and róuted,
thóse who hate Zíon!
6 Lét them be like gráss on the róof
that wíthers before it flówers.

7 With thát no réaper fills his árms,
no bínder makes his shéaves
8 and thóse passing bý will not sáy:
'On yóu the Lord's bléssing!'

'We bléss you in the náme òf the Lórd.'

129

Prayer of repentance and trust: sixth psalm of repentance

Waiting for the dawn of Israel's great deliverance. The psalmist, aware of his people's faithlessness, is equally sure of God's answer to repentance (cf. Neh. 1: 7-9). The return from exile was not yet 'full redemption'. Israel waited and prayed. She was still waiting when Simeon took a child in his arms and said: 'My eyes have seen thy salvation' (Lk. 2: 30). He held the infant Son of Man who came to give his life for the redemption of many (Mk. 10: 45)—'with the Lord, fullness of redemption'. But since this has come, how can we Christians still await it? How can we sing the psalm? Because though called we are not yet chosen, though heirs we do not yet enjoy the inheritance. Out of these depths our call must be constant and, if it is constant, it may be confident also. And there are some whose waiting is a purifying fire. This, more than any other, is their psalm.

FORMULA I 42

1 Out of the dépths I crý to you, O Lórd,
2 Lórd, hear my vóice!
O lét your éars be atténtive
to the vóice of my pléading.

3 If you, O Lórd, should márk our guílt,
Lórd, who would survíve?
4 But with yóu is fóund forgíveness:
for thís we revére you.

5 My sóul is wáiting for the Lórd,
I cóunt on his wórd.
6 My sóul is lónging for the Lórd
more than wátchman for dáybreak.
(Let the wátchman cóunt on dáybreak
7 and Ísrael on the Lórd.)

Becáuse with the Lórd there is mércy
and fúllness of redémption,
8 Ísrael indéed he will redéem
from áll its iníquity.

228

130

Song of serenity:
a pilgrimage song

A perfect expression of the childlike trust and peace which should be the attitude of the children of God. But not one that is achieved without effort —'I have set my soul in peace . . .'

FORMULA I 54

1 O Lórd, my héart is not próud
    nor háughty my éyes.
    I have not góne after thíngs too gréat
    nor márvels beyónd me.

2 Trúly I have sét my sóul
    in sílence and péace.
    A weaned chíld on its móther's bréast,
    even só is my sóul.

3 O Ísrael, hópe in the Lórd
    both nów and for éver.

131

God's promise to David:
a pilgrimage song

Our Lord, our king, came to bring God to earth. For this he worked with unwearying labour, with sweat and even with blood. And the result of his work was not a building, a Temple; but the Church, where God really does dwell, eternally.

FORMULA V 3

1 O Lórd, remémber Dávid
    and áll the many hárdships he endúred,
2 the óath he swóre to the Lórd,
    his vów to the Stróng One of Jácob.

3 'I will not énter the hóuse where I líve
nor gó to the béd where I rést.
4 I will gíve no sléep to my éyes
to my éyelids I will gíve no slúmber
5 till I fínd a pláce for the Lórd,
a dwélling for the Stróng One of Jácob.'

6 At Éphrata we héard of the árk;
we fóund it in the pláins of Yearím.
7 'Let us gó to the pláce of his dwélling;
let us gó to knéel at his fóotstool.'

8 Go up, Lórd, to the pláce of your rést,
yóu and the árk of your stréngth.
9 Your príests shall be clóthed with hóliness:
your fáithful shall ríng out their jóy.
10 For the sáke of Dávid your sérvant
dó not rejéct your anóinted.

11 The Lórd swore an óath to Dávid;
he wíll not go báck on his wórd:
'A són, the frúit of your bódy,
will I sét upón your thróne.

12 If they kéep my cóvenant in trúth
and my láws that Í have táught them,
their sóns álso shall rúle
on your thróne from áge to áge.'

13 For the Lórd has chósen Zíon;
he has desíred it fór his dwélling:
14 'Thís is my résting-place for éver,
hére have I chósen to líve.

15 I will gréatly bléss her próduce,
I will fíll her póor with bréad.
16 I will clóthe her príests with salvátion
and her fáithful shall ríng out their jóy.

17 Thére David's stóck will flówer:
I will prepáre a lámp for my anóinted.
18 I will cóver his énemies with sháme
but on hím my crówn shall shíne.'

132

The blessings of unity:
a pilgrimage song

*The dew which makes the barren soil fresh and green and fruitful is a
visible sign of God's blessing. Oil too is a symbol of the rich bounty of
God's love for us. But greater still is charity: 'Where two or three are
gathered together, there am I in the midst of them.'*

FORMULA I 52

1 How góod and how pléasant it ís,
   when bróthers líve in únity!

2 It is líke precious óil upon the héad
   running dówn upon the béard,
   running dówn upon Áaron's béard
   upon the cóllar of his róbes.

3 It is líke the dew of Hérmon which fálls
   on the héights of Zíon.
   For thére the Lórd gives his bléssing,
   life for éver.

133

Prayer at night-time:
a pilgrimage song

*God did not merely make the world by a single act—he is creating it
continually; and unending too is the hymn of praise which we voice for
creation.*

FORMULA V 23

1 O cóme, bléss the Lórd,
   all yóu who sérve the Lórd,
   who stánd in the hóuse of the Lórd,
   in the cóurts of the hóuse of our Gód.

2 Lift up your hánds to the hóly pláce
and bléss the Lórd through the níght.

3 May the Lórd bléss you from Zíon,   [omit B+c]
he who máde both héaven and éarth.

134

Anthology of praise

God, the living God, has cast out the prince of this world, has broken the power of the kingdom of evil, and formed for himself a holy nation, a kingdom of priests.

FORMULA V 17

1 Alleluia!

Práise the náme of the Lórd,
práise him, sérvants of the Lórd,
2 who stánd in the hóuse of the Lórd
in the cóurts of the hóuse of our Gód.

3 Praise the Lórd for the Lórd is góod.
Sing a psálm to his náme for he is lóving.
4 For the Lórd has chosen Jácob for himsélf
and Ísrael for his ówn posséssion.

5 For I knów the Lórd is gréat,
that our Lórd is hígh above all góds.
6 The Lórd does whatéver he wílls,
in héaven, on éarth, in the séas.

7 He summons clóuds from the énds of the éarth;
makes líghtning prodúce the ráin;
from his tréasuries he sénds forth the wínd.

8 The fírst-born of the Egýptians he smóte,
of mán and béast alíke.
9 Sígns and wónders he wórked
In the mídst of your lánd, O Égypt,
against Pháraoh and áll his sérvants.

10 Nátions in their gréatness he strúck
and kíngs in their spléndour he sléw.
11 Síhon, kíng of the Ámorites,
Óg, the kíng of Báshan,
and áll the kíngdoms of Cánaan.
12 He let Ísrael inhérit their lánd;
on his péople their lánd he bestówed.

13 Lórd, your náme stands for éver,
unforgótten from áge to áge:
14 for the Lórd does jústice for his péople;
the Lórd takes píty on his sérvants.

15 Pagan ídols are sílver and góld,
the wórk of húman hánds.
16 They have móuths but they cánnot spéak;
they have éyes but they cánnot sée.

17 They have éars but they cánnot héar;
there is néver a bréath on their líps.
18 Their mákers will come to bé like thém
and so will áll who trúst in thém!

19 Sons of Ísrael, bléss the Lórd!
Sons of Áaron, bléss the Lórd!
20 Sons of Lévi, bléss the Lórd!
You who féar him, bléss the Lórd!

21 From Zíon may the Lórd be bléssed,
hé who dwélls in Jerúsalem!

135

Litany of praises: psalm of worship

A 'Te Deum' to the master of creation who delivers the people he has chosen. Egypt felt his power, Sihon of the Transjordanian mountains, Og of the further north. By their downfall God made Israel's name dreaded in Canaan (Jos. 2: 10), the land that fell to her as her 'inheritance'. But military conquest was only an early stage in God's plan for all his world. We who have seen the design unfold are little moved by the psalmist's lesser joy. 'Inheritance of the land', classical formula of Israel's ideal, was a hope gradually purified, indeed, and spiritualized by national misfortune; taken into our Lord's hands it was blessed and changed for ever. 'The meek shall possess the land', not the warlike; the Kingdom is not of this world. Nor is the conquest: Pharaoh, Og, Sihon are foes within us, for our war is with the rulers of this darkness. Our armour is the apparel of the spirit (Eph. 6: 12ff). Thank God for his victorious grace, and for 'an inheritance that cannot fade, reserved in heaven' (1 Pet. 1: 4).

FORMULA PS 24

1 Alleluia!
O give thánks to the Lórd for he is góod,
for his lóve endúres for éver.*

2 Give thánks to the Gód of góds,
for his lóve endúres for éver.

3 Give thánks to the Lórd of lórds,
for his lóve endúres for éver;

4 who alóne has wrought márvellous wórks,
for his lóve endúres for éver;

5 whose wísdom it wás made the skíes,
for his lóve endúres for éver;

6 who fíxed the earth fírmly on the séas,
for his lóve endúres for éver.

7 It was hé who máde the great líghts,
for his lóve endúres for éver,

8 the sún to rúle in the dáy,
for his lóve endúres for éver,

9 the móon and stárs in the níght,
for his lóve endúres for éver.

10 The first-bórn of the Egýptians he smóte,
for his lóve endúres for éver.

11 He brought Ísrael óut from their mídst,
for his lóve endúres for éver;

12 arm outstrétched, with pówer in his hánd,
for his lóve endúres for éver.

* In the musical editions of the above psalm the refrain appears as a paraphrase: 'Great is his love, love without end.'

13 He divíded the Réd Sea in twó,
for his lóve endúres for éver;
14 he made Ísrael páss through the mídst,
for his lóve endúres for éver;
15 he flung Pháraoh and his fórce in the séa,
for his lóve endúres for éver.

16 Through the désert his péople he léd,
for his lóve endúres for éver.
17 Nátions in their gréatness he strúck,
for his lóve endúres for éver.
18 Kíngs in their spléndour he sléw,
for his lóve endúres for éver.

19 Síhon, kíng of the Ámorites,
for his lóve endúres for éver;
20 and Óg, the kíng of Báshan,
for his lóve endúres for éver.

21 He let Ísrael inhérit their lánd,
for his lóve endúres for éver.
22 On his sérvant their lánd he bestówed,
for his lóve endúres for éver.
23 He remémbered ús in our distréss,
for his lóve endúres for éver.

24 And he snátched us awáy from our fóes,
for his lóve endúres for éver.
25 He gives fóod to áll living thíngs,
for his lóve endúres for éver.
26 To the Gód of héaven give thánks,
for his lóve endúres for éver.

136

Homesickness in exile

A Christian cannot feel entirely at home in a world where religion is just a matter of mild curiosity, or even an object of violent attack. But we will not succumb, we will not forget what people we are; nor will we just wait passively for the end, but vigorously repel the attacks to which the Church is subject.

1 By the rívers of Bábylon
  thére we sat and wépt,
  remémbering Zíon;
2 on the póplars that gréw there
  we húng up our hárps.

3 For it was thére that they ásked us,
  our cáptors, for sóngs,
  our oppréssors, for jóy.
  'Síng to us,' they sáid,
  'one of Zíon's sóngs.'

4 O hów could we síng
  the sóng of the Lórd
  on álien sóil?
5 If I forgét you, Jerúsalem,
  let my ríght hand wíther!

6 O lét my tóngue
  cléave to my móuth
  if I remémber you nót,
  if I príze not Jerúsalem
  abóve all my jóys!

7 Remémber, O Lórd,
  against the sóns of Édom
  the dáy of Jerúsalem;
  when they sáid: 'Tear it dówn!
  Tear it dówn to its foundátions!'

8 O Bábylon, destróyer,
  he is háppy who repáys you
  the ílls you brought on ús.
9 He shall séize and shall dásh
  your chíldren on the róck!

137

Thanksgiving to a faithful God

The great God, lord of the world and of angels, cares for us, constantly surpassing what we could expect from him.

FORMULA II 24

1 I thánk you, Lórd, with all my héart,
you have héard the wórds of my móuth.
In the présence of the ángels I will bléss you.
2 I will adóre before your hóly témple.

I thánk you for your fáithfulness and lóve
which excél all we éver knew of yóu.
3 On the dáy I cálled, you ánswered;
you incréased the stréngth of my sóul.

4 Áll earth's kíngs shall thánk you
when they héar the wórds of your móuth.
5 They shall síng of the Lórd's wáys:
'How gréat is the glóry of the Lórd!'

6 The Lord is hígh yet he lóoks on the lówly
and the háughty he knóws from afár.
7 Though I wálk in the mídst of afflíction
you give me lífe and frustráte my fóes.

You strétch out your hánd and sáve me,
your hánd *8* will do áll things for mé.
Your lóve, O Lórd, is etérnal,
discárd not the wórk of your hánds.

138

The Hound of Heaven

Our thoughts may sweep and soar over all the world, over the bewildering profusion of the galaxies, and know that God is there, wherever our mind's eye looks—and that he is also in the depths of our own soul.

FORMULA V 23

1 O Lórd, you séarch me and you knów me,　　[omit D]
2 you knów my résting and my rísing,
　you discérn my púrpose from afár.
3 You márk when I wálk or lie dówn,
　all my wáys lie ópen to yóu.

4 Before éver a wórd is on my tóngue
　you knów it, O Lórd, through and thróugh.
5 Behínd and befóre you besíege me,
　your hánd ever láid upón me.　　[repeat D]
6 Too wónderful for mé, this knówledge,
　too hígh, beyónd my réach.

7 O whére can I gó from your spírit,　　[omit G+D]
　or whére can I flée from your fáce?
8 If I clímb the héavens, you are thére.
　If I líe in the gráve, you are thére.

9 If I táke the wíngs of the dáwn
　and dwéll at the séa's furthest énd,
10 even thére your hánd would léad me,
　your ríght hand would hóld me fást.

11 If I sáy: 'Let the dárkness híde me
　and the líght aróund me be níght,'
12 even dárkness is not dárk for yóu
　and the níght is as cléar as the dáy.

13 For it was yóu who creáted my béing,
　knit me togéther in my móther's wómb.
14 I thánk you for the wónder of my béing,
　for the wónders of áll your creátion.

Alréady you knéw my sóul,
15 my bódy held no sécret from yóu
when Í was being fáshioned in sécret
and móulded in the dépths of the éarth.

16 Your éyes saw áll my áctions,
they were áll of them wrítten in your bóok;
every óne of my dáys was decréed
before óne of them cáme into béing.

17 To mé, how mystérious your thóughts,
the súm of them nót to be númbered!

18 If I cóunt them, they are móre than the sánd;
to fínish, I must be etérnal, like yóu.

19 O Gód, that you would sláy the wícked!
Men of blóod, keep fár awáy from me!

20 With decéit they rebél agáinst you
and sét your desígns at náught.

21 Do I not háte thóse who háte you,
abhór those who ríse agáinst you?

22 I háte them with a pérfect háte
and théy are fóes to mé.

23 O séarch me, Gód, and know my héart.
O tést me and knów my thóughts.

24 See that I fóllow not the wróng páth
and léad me in the páth of life etérnal.

139

Prayer under persecution

*The life of man on earth is a warfare; there can be no truce between our
Lord and the prince of darkness, and men must take sides. Here we take
our side, knowing that the battle is bitter but the victory certain.*

FORMULA V 9

2 Réscue me, Lórd, from evil mén;
from the víolent kéep me sáfe,

239

3 from thóse who plan évil in their héarts
and stír up strífe every dáy;
4 who shárpen their tóngue like an ádder's,
with the póison of víper on their líps.

5 Lord, guárd me from the hánds of the wícked;
from the víolent kéep me sáfe;
they plán to máke me stúmble.
6 The próud have hídden a tráp,
have spréad out línes in a nét,
set snáres acróss my páth.

7 I have sáid to the Lórd: 'You are my Gód.'
Lord, héar the crý of my appéal!
8 Lord my Gód, my míghty hélp,
you shíeld my héad in the báttle.
9 Do not gránt the wícked their desíre
nor lét their plóts succéed.

10 Those surróunding me lift up their héads.
Let the málice of their spéech overwhélm them.
11 Let cóals of fíre rain upón them.
Let them be flúng in the abýss, no more to ríse.
12 Let the slánderer not endúre upon the éarth.
Let évil hunt the víolent man to déath!

13 I know the Lórd will avénge the póor,
that hé will do jústice for the néedy.
Yes, the júst will práise your náme:
the úpright shall líve in your présence.

140

Evening prayer for protection

*As each day ends, what have we to bring to God? Only our weariness
with the struggle, our dismay that it must continue, and our prayer that
we may persevere.*

1 I have cálled to you, Lórd; hásten to hélp me!
Héar my vóice when I crý to yóu.

2 Let my práyer aríse befóre you like íncense,
the ráising of my hánds like an évening oblátion.

3 Sét, O Lórd, a guard óver my móuth;
keep wátch, O Lórd, at the dóor of my líps!

4 Do not túrn my héart to thíngs that are wróng,
to évil déeds with mén who are sínners.

Néver allów me to sháre in their féasting.
5 If a góod man stríkes or repróves me it is kíndness;
but let the óil of the wícked not anóint my héad.
Let my práyer be éver agáinst their málice.

6 Their prínces were thrown dówn by the síde of the
róck:
thén they understóod that my wórds were kínd.
7 As a míllstone is sháttered to píeces on the gróund,
so their bónes were stréwn at the móuth of the gráve.

8 To yóu, Lord Gód, my éyes are túrned:
in yóu I take réfuge; spáre my sóul!
9 From the tráp they have láid for me kéep me sáfe:
kéep me from the snáres of thóse who do évil.

10 Let the wícked fáll into the tráps they have sét
whilst Í pursúe my wáy unhármed.

141

Prayer of a man deserted by his friends

*The feeling of failure comes to everyone at some time: the feeling of
desolation when things go wrong, when friends fail, when every escape
route seems barred aud we have nowhere to turn except in on ourselves:
but it is then that we find that there is always God, who knows and cares.*

2 With all my vóice I crý to the Lórd,
　　with all my vóice I entréat the Lórd.
3 I póur out my tróuble befóre him;
　　I téll him áll my distréss
4 while my spírit fáints withín me.
　　But yóu, O Lórd, know my páth.

　　On the wáy where Í shall wálk
　　they have hídden a snáre to entráp me.
5 Lóok on my ríght and sée:
　　there is nó one who tákes my párt.
　　I have nó meáns of escápe,
　　not óne who cáres for my sóul.

6 I crý to yóu, O Lórd.　　　　　　　　　　[omit D]
　　I have sáid: 'Yóu are my réfuge,
　　all I háve in the lánd of the líving.'
7 Lísten, thén, to my crý
　　for Í am in the dépths of distréss.

　　Réscue me from thóse who pursúe me
　　for théy are strónger than Í.
8 Bríng my sóul out of this príson
　　and thén I shall práise your náme.
　　Aróund me the júst will assémble
　　becáuse of your góodness to mé.

142

Prayer in desolation:
seventh psalm of repentance

We do not always find it possible to connect a particular suffering with a
specific sin, but it is true that human suffering is the mark of our estrange-
ment from God; and in our sorrow we become aware of that gulf, and
aware therefore of our desperate need of him.

1 Lórd, lísten to my práyer: [omit D]
túrn your éar to my appéal.
You are fáithful, you are júst; give ánswer.
2 Do not cáll your sérvant to júdgment
for nó one is júst in your síght.

3 The énemy pursúes my sóul;
he has crúshed my lífe to the gróund;
he has máde me dwéll in dárkness
like the déad, lóng forgótten.
4 Thérefore my spírit fáils;
my héart is númb withín me.

5 I remémber the dáys that are pást: [omit D]
I pónder áll your wórks.
I múse on what your hánd has wróught
6 and to yóu I strétch out my hánds.
Like a párched land my sóul thirsts for yóu.

7 Lórd, make háste and ánswer;   [omit D+E]
for my spírit fáils withín me.
Dó not híde your fáce
lest I becóme like thóse in the gráve.

8 In the mórning let me knów your lóve   [omit D+E]
for I pút my trúst in yóu.
Make me knów the wáy I should wálk:
to yóu I líft up my sóul.

9 Réscue me, Lórd, from my énemies;
I have fléd to yóu for réfuge.
10 Téach me to dó your wíll
for yóu, O Lórd, are my Gód.
Let yóur good spírit guíde me
in wáys that are lével and smóoth.

11 For your náme's sake, Lórd, save my lífe;   [omit D]
in your jústice save my sóul from distréss.
12 In your lóve make an énd of my fóes;
destróy all thóse who oppréss me
for Í am your sérvant, O Lórd.

243

143

Appeal for victory and peace

*Our Lord, the son of man, shared our weakness, shared our struggle; but
in doing so he showed us that God's strength shows itself most clearly in
our weakness, bringing us joy and salvation.*

FORMULA V 23

1 Bléssed be the Lórd, my róck   [omit c+d+e]
   who tráins my árms for báttle,
   who prepáres my hánds for wár.

2 Hé is my lóve, my fórtress;   [omit d+e]
   hé is my strónghold, my sáviour,
   my shíeld, my pláce of réfuge.
   He brings péoples únder my rúle.

3 Lórd, what is mán that you cáre for him,   [omit d+e]
   mortal mán, that you kéep him in mínd;
4 mán, who is mérely a bréath
   whose lífe fádes like a shádow?

5 Lówer your héavens and come down;   [omit d+e]
   touch the móuntains; wréathe them in smóke.
6 Flash your líghtnings; róut the fóe,
   shoot your árrows and pút them to flíght.

7 Reach dówn from héaven and sáve me;   [omit d]
   draw me óut from the míghty wáters,
   from the hánds of álien fóes
8 whose móuths are fílled with líes,
   whose hánds are ráised in pérjury.

9 To you, O Gód, will I síng a new sóng;   [omit d+e]
   I will pláy on the tén-stringed lúte
10 to yóu who give kíngs their víctory,
   who set Dávid your sérvant frée.

11 You set him frée from the évil swórd;   [omit D+E]
    you réscued him from álien fóes
    whose móuths were fílled with líes,
    whose hánds were ráised in pérjury.

*   *   *

12 Let our sóns then flóurish like sáplings   [omit D+E]
    grown táll and stróng from their yóuth:
    our dáughters gráceful as cólumns,
    adórned as thóugh for a pálace.

13 Let our bárns be fílled to overflówing   [omit D]
    with cróps of évery kínd;
    our shéep incréasing by thóusands,
    mýriads of shéep in our fíelds,
14 our cáttle héavy with yóung,

    no rúined wáll, no éxile,   [omit D+E]
    no sóund of wéeping in our stréets.
15 Háppy the péople with such bléssings;
    happy the péople whose Gód is the Lórd.

144

Praise of God's grandeur: an alphabetical psalm

When we reflect on what God has done for us, we remember that this is what God has always done; our lives are borne along on the unending stream of divine love. To the eternal God, eternal praise be given.

FORMULA II 24

1 I will give you glóry, O Gód my Kíng,
    I will bléss your náme for éver.

2 I will bléss you dáy after dáy
    and práise your náme for éver.
3 The Lord is gréat, híghly to be práised,
    his gréatness cánnot be méasured.

4 Age to áge shall procláim your wórks,
   shall decláre your míghty déeds,
5 shall spéak of your spléndour and glóry,
   tell the tále of your wónderful wórks.
6 They will spéak of your térrible déeds,
   recóunt your gréatness and míght.
7 They will recáll your abúndant góodness;
   age to áge shall ríng out your jústice.

8 The Lord is kínd and fúll of compássion,
   slow to ánger, abóunding in lóve.
9 How góod is the Lórd to áll,
   compássionate to áll his créatures.

10 All your créatures shall thánk you, O Lórd,
    and your fríends shall repéat their bléssing.
11 They shall spéak of the glóry of your réign
    and decláre your míght, O Gód,

12 to make knówn to mén your mighty déeds
    and the glórious spléndour of your réign.
13 Yóurs is an éverlasting kíngdom;
    your rúle lasts from áge to áge.

    The Lord is fáithful in áll his wórds
    and lóving in áll his déeds.
14 The Lórd suppórts all who fáll
    and ráises áll who are bowed dówn.

15 The éyes of all créatures look to yóu
    and you gíve them their fóod in due tíme.
16 You ópen wíde your hánd,
    grant the desíres of áll who líve.

17 The Lord is júst in áll his wáys
    and lóving in áll his déeds.
18 He is clóse to áll who cáll him,
    who cáll on hím from their héarts.

19 He gránts the desíres of those who féar him,
    he héars their crý and he sáves them.
20 The Lórd protécts all who lóve him;
    but the wícked he will útterly destróy.

21 Let me spéak the práise of the Lórd,   [omit B]
let all mankínd bléss his holy náme
for éver, for áges unénding.

145

Praise of God's fidelity

*The Almighty God is at our service: the All-Mighty, the only mighty;
we cannot take out a second insurance—we must rely on him only, cast
all our care on the Lord for he has care of us.*

FORMULA V 30 (A+B+C+D)

1 Alleluia!

My sóul, give práise to the Lórd;   [omit c]
2 I will práise the Lórd all my dáys,
make músic to my Gód while I líve.

3 Pút no trúst in prínces,
in mortal mén in whóm there is no hélp.
4 Take their bréath, they retúrn to cláy
and their pláns that dáy come to nóthing.

5 He is háppy who is hélped by Jacob's Gód,
whose hópe is in the Lórd his Gód,
6 who alóne made héaven and éarth,
the séas and áll they contáin.

It is hé who keeps fáith for éver,
7 who is júst to thóse who are oppréssed.
It is hé who gives bréad to the húngry,
the Lórd, who sets prísoners frée,

8 the Lórd who gives síght to the blínd,
who ráises up thóse who are bowed dówn,
9 the Lórd, who protécts the stránger
and uphólds the wídow and órphan.

8c It is the Lórd who lóves the júst
9c but thwárts the páth of the wícked.
10 The Lórd will réign for éver,
Zion's Gód, from áge to áge.

Alleluia!

146

Praise to God who maintains the world

God knows each of the myriad stars, not a sparrow falls without his knowing, the hairs of our head are numbered. He does not want us to try to rival him in power, but simply to wait on his love for us.

FORMULA V 30 (A+B+C+D)

1 Alleluia!

Praise the Lórd for hé is góod;   [omit c]
sing to our Gód for hé is lóving:
to hím our práise is dúe.

2 The Lórd buílds up Jerúsalem   [V 30+E+F]
and bríngs back Ísrael's éxiles,
3 he héals the bróken-héarted,
he bínds up áll their wóunds.
4 He fíxes the númber of the stárs;
he cálls each óne by its náme.

5 Our Lórd is gréat and almíghty;
his wísdom can néver be méasured.
6 The Lórd ráises the lówly;
he húmbles the wícked to the dúst.
7 O síng to the Lórd, giving thánks;
sing psálms to our Gód with the hárp.

8 He cóvers the héavens with clóuds;
he prepáres the ráin for the éarth,
making móuntains spróut with gráss
and with plánts to sérve man's néeds.

248

9 He provídes the béasts with their fóod
and young rávens that cáll upón him.

10 His delíght is nót in hórses
nor his pléasure in wárriors' stréngth.
11 The Lórd delights in thóse who revére him,
in thóse who wáit for his lóve.

147

Praise of God's personal care for Israel

In the beginning was the word, creating all things, and even upsetting things—like changing running water to solid ice, or making snow fall in the hot land of Palestine! And he can change us too: the Word of God, Jesus Christ, shows us God's will; he is the Way, leading us from misery to peace and happiness.

FORMULA II 31

12 O práise the Lórd, Jerúsalem!
Zíon, práise your Gód!

13 He has stréngthened the bárs of your gátes,
he has bléssed the chíldren withín you.
14 He estáblished péace on your bórders,
he féeds you with fínest whéat.

15 He sénds out his wórd to the éarth
and swíftly rúns his commánd.
16 He shówers down snów white as wóol,
he scátters hóar-frost like áshes.

17 He húrls down háilstones like crúmbs.
The wáters are frózen at his tóuch;
18 he sénds forth his wórd and it mélts them:
at the bréath of his móuth the waters flów.

19 He mákes his wórd known to Jácob,
to Ísrael his láws and decrées.

20 He has not déalt thus with óther nátions;
he has not táught them hís decrées.

Alleluia!

148

Cosmic praise

The whole of creation resounds with the praise of God; the music begins in heaven, and from there passes down to earth and goes round the whole world. But at the centre of it all is the people of God. For they are the beginning of a new creàtion, and through them the whole world is to be recreated, to the greater glory of God.

FORMULA PS 20

1 Alleluia!

Práise the Lórd from the héavens,
práise him in the héights.
2 Práise him, all his ángels,
práise him, áll his hóst.

3 Práise him, sún and móon,
práise him, shining stárs.
4 Práise him, highest héavens
and the wáters abóve the héavens.

5 Let them práise the náme of the Lórd.
He commánded: they were máde.
6 He fíxed them for éver,
gave a láw which shall nót pass awáy.

7 Práise the Lórd from the éarth,
séa creatures and all óceans,
8 fire and háil, snow and míst,
stormy wínds that obéy his wórd;

9 áll móuntains and hílls,
all frúit trees and cédars,
10 béasts, wild and táme,
réptiles and bírds on the wíng;

250

11 áll earth's kíngs and péoples,
earth's prínces and rúlers;
12 yóung men and máidens,
old men togéther with chíldren.

13 Let them práise the náme of the Lórd
for he alóne is exálted.
The spléndour of his náme
réaches beyond héaven and éarth.

14 He exálts the stréngth of his péople.
He is the práise of all his sáints,
of the sóns of Ísrael,
of the péople to whóm he comes clóse.

Alleluia!

149

Praise to the God of victories

We join in the song of victory, the triumph of God, the crushing of the serpent's head; for we have our part in this victorious struggle, wearing the armour of God, the helmet of salvation and the sword of the spirit.

FORMULA V 17

1 Alleluia!

Síng a new sóng to the Lórd,
his práise in the assémbly of the fáithful.
2 Let Ísrael rejóice in its Máker,
let Zíon's sons exúlt in their kíng.
3 Let them práise his náme with dáncing
and make músic with tímbrel and hárp.

4 For the Lórd takes delíght in his péople.
He crówns the póor with salvátion.
5 Let the fáithful rejóice in their glóry,
shout for jóy and táke their rést.

6 Let the práise of Gód be on their líps
and a twó-edged swórd in their hánd,

7 to déal out véngeance to the nátions
and púnishment on áll the péoples;
8 to bínd their kíngs in cháins
and their nóbles in fétters of íron;
9 to cárry out the séntence pre-ordáined:
this hónour is for áll his fáithful.

Alleluia!

150

Final summons to praise

The psalms have shown us prayers of petition, lament, instruction, warning and exhortation: but above all and in all they are praises of God. This praise will more and more absorb our being, absorb every being, in a final diapason.

FORMULA II 18

1 Alleluia!

Práise Gód in his hóly pláce,
práise him in his míghty héavens.
2 Práise him for his pówerful déeds,
práise his surpássing gréatness.

3 O práise him with sóund of trúmpet,
práise him with lúte and hárp.
4 Práise him with tímbrel and dánce,
práise him with stríngs and pípes.

5 O práise him with resóunding cýmbals,
práise him with cláshing of cýmbals.
6 Let éverything that líves and that bréathes
give práise to the Lórd. Allelúia!

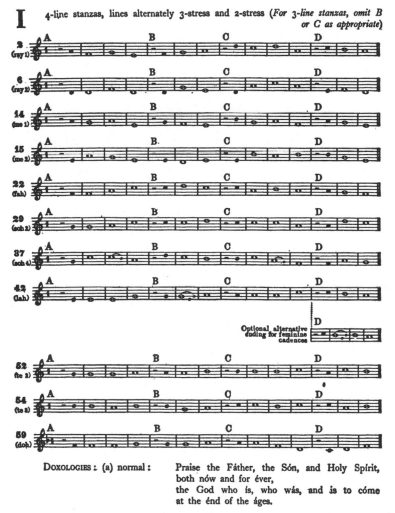

I 4-line stanzas, lines alternately 3-stress and 2-stress (*For 3-line stanzas, omit B or C as appropriate*)

Optional alternative ending for feminine cadences

DOXOLOGIES: (a) normal: Praise the Fáther, the Són, and Holy Spírit,
both nów and for éver,
the God who ís, who wás, and is to cóme
at the énd of the áges.

(b) short form*:   Praise the Fáther, the Són and Holy Spírit
for éver and éver.

* The shorter doxology is used at the end of a psalm when its final stanza
has only 2 lines and needs to be completed by the addition of 2 more lines.

II 4-line stanzas, 3-stress lines (*For 3-line stanzas, omit the section marked .*)

DOXOLOGIES : (a) normal :
Give práise to the Fáther Almíghty,
to his Són, Jesus Chríst the Lórd,
to the Spírit who dwélls in our héarts,
both nów and for éver. Amén.

(b) short form*: To the Fáther, the Són and Holy Spírit
give práise for éver. Amén.

* The shorter doxology is used at the end of a psalm when its final stanza
has only 2 lines and needs to be completed by the addition of 2 more lines.

III 4-line stanzas, 4-stress lines (*For 3-line stanzas, omit the section marked **)

12
(me)

26
(soph 1)

34
(soh 2)

49
(te 1)

DOXOLOGY   Give práise to the Fáther, the Són and Holy Spírit
(sung to sections A and D): both nów and for áges unénding. Amén.

IV 6-line stanzas, lines alternately 3-stress and 2-stress (*If the stanza is a line short, omit the corresponding section. For irregular stanzas of 4 lines, omit the sections between ⌐ and ¬*)

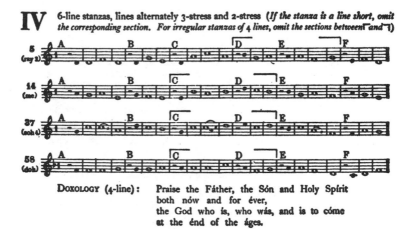

5
(ray 1)

14
(me)

37
(soh 4)

58
(doh)

DOXOLOGY (4-line):   Praise the Fáther, the Són and Holy Spírit
both nów and for éver,
the God who ís, who wás, and is to cóme
at the énd of the áges.

V

6-line stanzas, 4-stress lines (*For 5-line stanzas, omit the section marked* *. *For 4-line stanzas, omit the sections between* ⌐ *and* ⌐)

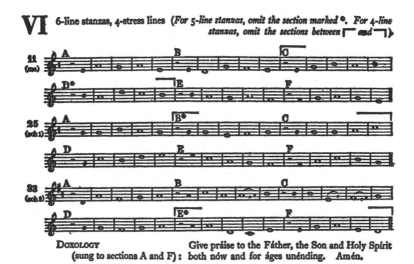

DOXOLOGY (4-line):

Give práise to the Fáther Almíghty,
to his Són, Jesus Christ the Lórd,
to the Spírit who dwélls in our héarts,
both nów and for éver. Amén.

VI

6-line stanzas, 4-stress lines (*For 5-line stanzas, omit the section marked* *. *For 4-line stanzas, omit the sections between* ⌐ *and* ⌐)

DOXOLOGY
(sung to sections A and F):

Give práise to the Fáther, the Son and Holy Spírit
both nów and for áges unénding. Amén.